W9-DGC-381

BALDESAR CASTIGLIONE

The Book of
THE COURTIER

Translated and edited by

FRIENCH SIMPSON
San Jose State College

UNGAR • NEW YORK

MILESTONES
OF THOUGHT
in the History of Ideas

General Editors
F. W. STROTHMANN
FREDERICK W. LOCKE
Stanford University

Eleventh Printing, 1987

Copyright © 1959 by
The Ungar Publishing Company

Printed in the United States of America

Library of Congress Catalog Card No. 59-15520

ISBN 0-8044-6078-7

INTRODUCTION

COUNT BALDESAR CASTIGLIONE was born at Casatico in the territory of Mantua, December 6, 1478. His education included the study of Latin and Greek and was rounded out by a sojourn at the court of Ludovico Sforza at Milan and by military service with the Marquess of Mantua on an expedition to aid the French in Naples. After the defeat of the Marquess in 1503, Castiglione entered the service of Duke Guid'Ubaldo (or Guidobaldo) da Montefeltro and took up residence at the court of Urbino. At the death of the duke, Castiglione served the duke's nephew and heir, Francesco Maria della Rovere. In 1513 Castiglione was made ambassador from Urbino to the papal court in Rome and later became ambassador from Mantua. In 1524 Pope Clement VII sent Castiglione to Spain as Papal Nuncio to the Emperor Charles V. Three years later the capture and sack of Rome by the Imperial forces took place, and Castiglione found himself charged by the Pope with negligence and credulity in dealing with the Emperor. He died at Toledo, February 7, 1529, one week after the Emperor had appointed him Bishop of Avila.

In his dedicatory letter to *The Book of the Courtier,* Castiglione indicates that he composed his book shortly after the death of Duke Guidobaldo in 1508, though he probably worked at it until 1518. In Spain Castiglione learned that Vittoria della Colonna, to whom he had given a manuscript copy, had broken a promise to him by allowing a portion of the book to be copied out and that several versions of this portion were being circulated at Naples. In order to forestall the printing of unauthorized versions such as these, Castiglione himself ordered the book to be printed, and it appeared in Venice in 1528.

In Book One, Castiglione states that he was absent on a mission to England when the supposed dialogues took place.

In reality he returned to Urbino at the time of Pope Julius II's visit in March, 1507. The fiction of his absence merely reflects the compunction authors generally have felt about appearing as speakers in their own dialogues.

The powerful interest which Castiglione's book held for his contemporaries doubtless lay in the fact that it clearly recognized the existence of what was in reality a new social type—the Courtier or, more broadly, the gentleman, into which the knight of the Middle Ages had developed under the influence of the political institutions and humanistic culture of the Renaissance. *The Courtier* was intended primarily to depict the attributes which the ideal courtier or gentleman should possess, but it goes far afield in debating political, moral, and artistic issues raised incidentally in the course of the discussion. For example, the following questions are debated: Is it necessary or not that the Courtier be of noble birth? Should he regard arms or letters as his chief profession or ornament? What vocabulary should the Courtier favor in speaking and writing in the vulgar tongue? Is the perfection of Courtiership an end in itself, or must it serve some further end in order to be worthy? Can an older Courtier be a lover, or must he renounce love? Some of the questions not specifically concerned with the attributes of the Courtier are the following: Is painting or sculpture the more admirable art? Are virtues innate or acquired? In choice do we always choose what we think is good, or do we sometimes choose the bad knowing it to be bad? Is a monarchy or a republic the better form of government? Whatever the position favored by Castiglione in these matters, there is one doctrine which we may be sure he favored: that whatever the Courtier does he must do with grace. Grace springs chiefly from *sprezzatura,* which is an air of perfect naturalness acquired through discipline. The motto of the Courtier is, then, *Ars est celare artem,* and we find that this motto forms the basis of the character of the gentleman in succeeding centuries and indeed may be taken as the basis of aristocratic manners in all periods.

If this *sprezzatura* looks back to the *urbanitas* of writers like Horace, the morality of the Courtier looks back to the four components of Cicero's *honestas,* while the framework for the courtier's sentiments on love is supplied by the tradition of Courtly Love and by Renaissance Platonism.

The Courtier, therefore, mirrors a fundamental Renaissance trait, one clearly foreshadowed in Petrarch: the search for a fine human personality and culture, in a word, *humanitas,* to be achieved in large measure through the study and imitation of antiquity. It is a way of life rather than a theological, metaphysical, or ethical doctrine that interests Castiglione and his contemporaries. In *The Courtier,* then, we find essentially the same views that Erasmus and Rabelais urged against Medieval conceptions of education and character.

Within the compass of this volume it has been possible to include only those passages of *The Courtier* which set forth the basic doctrines of the work, with such additional material as seemed requisite to a just conception of the work's range and method. Much has had to be omitted. The content of omitted passages has been given in summary wherever space allowed. Section numerals have been retained to facilitate comparison with the original, as well as to indicate what has been omitted. Cuts within sentences and paragraphs have been indicated in the conventional fashion.

F.S.

BIBLIOGRAPHICAL NOTE

Castiglione, Baldesar. *Opere volgari e latine del conte Baldesar Castiglione novellamente raccolte, ordinate, ricorrette e illustrate da G. Ant. e Gaetano Volpi, Padova,* Comino, 1733.

————— *Il Libro del Cortegiano del Conte Baldesar Castiglione,* a cura di Vittorio Cian, quarta edizione riveduta e corretta, Sansoni, Firenze, 1946.

————— *The Book of the Courtier,* tr. Thomas Hoby, 1561.

————— *The Book of the Courtier,* tr. Leonard Eckstein Opdycke, New York, Horace Liveright, 1929.

The present translation is based on the edition by Vittorio Cian.

SPEAKERS IN *THE COURTIER* WHO APPEAR IN THESE SELECTIONS

1. PIETRO BEMBO (1470-1547). A learned humanist and Platonist, he lived at the court of Urbino from 1505 to 1511; afterwards he became a papal secretary, a cardinal, and Bishop of Gubbio and Bergamo.

2. LUDOVICO DA CANOSSA (1476-1532). A kinsman of Castiglione's, he lived at the court of Urbino for some years after 1496. In 1511 he became Bishop of Tricarico.

3. BERNARD DOVIZI, called Bibbiena from his birthplace (1470-1520). He was of humble parentage, but his wit and skill in diplomacy endeared him to his patrons, the Medici, and Pope Leo X (Giovanni de' Medici) made him Cardinal of Santa Maria in Portico.

4. FEDERICO FREGOSO (1480-1541). Educated at Urbino, he became Bishop of Gubbio. While his brother was Doge of Genoa he commanded first the army and afterwards the navy of Genoa. Toward the end of his life he became a cardinal.

5. OTTAVIANO FREGOSO (d. 1524). Expelled from Genoa, he was received at the court of Urbino in 1497. In 1513 he returned to Genoa and was elected Doge. In 1522 he was again expelled when the Imperial troops captured the city.

6. CESARE GONZAGA (c. 1475-1512). He was a cousin of Castiglione and like Castiglione was trained in arms, arts, and diplomacy.

7. ELIZABETTA GONZAGA (1471-1526), wife of Guidobaldo da Montefeltro, Duke of Urbino. Married to an invalid, childless, twice forced into exile from Urbino, she seems to have merited the praises which contemporaries gave her for fidelity to her husband, ability in handling the affairs of the duchy when occasion demanded, and personal charm.

8. GIULIANO DE' MEDICI (1479-1516). During tne exile of his family from Florence (1494-1512) he spent much time at Urbino, where a wing of the palace was reserved for his use. He

married an aunt of Francis I of France, who made him Duke of Nemours. He is remembered today largely because of the figure on his tomb in Florence, executed by Michelangelo.

9. MORELLO DA ORTONA. Little is known of him except that he was an elderly courtier in the service of the Duke of Urbino.

10. GASPAR (GASPARO) PALLAVICINO (1486-1511). A friend of Castiglione and of Bembo, he appears in *The Courtier* as a sharp-witted and sharp-tongued contemner of women.

11. EMILIA PIA (d. 1528). She was the widow of Guidobaldo's illegitimate brother and the inseparable companion of the Duchess Elisabetta. Her wit and discretion are praised by others besides Castiglione.

12. JOANNI CRISTOFORO ROMANO. (c. 1465-1512). He was an excellent sculptor, medalist, architect, and musician and is known to have been in Urbino at the time when the discourses of *The Courtier* are supposed to have taken place.

CONTENTS

BOOK ONE

The Attributes of the Perfect Courtier

*1. Castiglione undertakes the book at the instance
of his friend, Alfonso Ariosto.*

For a long time, dearest Messer Alfonso, I have debated
with myself which would be more difficult for me: to refuse
you what you have many times asked of me with such
insistence, or to do it. For on the one hand, I thought it
very ungenerous to refuse anything, and especially anything
commendable, to someone whom I love very deeply and by
whom I believe myself to be deeply loved; yet on the other
hand, I thought that to undertake a task without knowing
whether or not I could carry it out was not becoming a man
who regards just criticism as seriously as it ought to be
regarded. Finally, after much thought, I determined in this
instance to find out by trial how much assistance that affection and keen desire to please which, in other things, is
accustomed to increase so greatly the industry of men, might
lend to my diligence.

You ask me, then, to set down what in my opinion is
the concept of Courtiership which is best suited to a gentleman who resides at the court of princes and by means of
which he may gain the requisite ability and knowledge
to serve princes consummately in every reasonable matter,
receiving favor from them and praise from other men—in
short, what sort of man he should be who deserves to be
called a *perfect* Courtier, one not deficient in any respect.
Wherefore, when I considered this request of yours, I declare that, if I had not felt it a greater reproach to have
you regard me as weak in affection than to have others
regard me as weak in wit, I would have shunned this task
because I feared that I should be held rash by all who
know how difficult it is to select the most perfect concept,
and, as it were, the flower of this Courtiership from such a

1

variety of practices as those in use in the courts of Christendom. For custom often makes the same things please and displease us; and from this it sometimes results that customs, habits, ceremonies, and conventions which are esteemed at one time become unseemly; and in contrary manner the unseemly become esteemed. Therefore we clearly see that custom has greater power than reason to introduce new things among us and to efface those of long standing, so that the man who seeks to decide what constitutes perfection in these things often is deceived.

So then let us at last make a beginning of our subject, and if possible let us fashion a Courtier such that the prince who is worthy of being served by him may be called a very noble lord though possessed only of a small state. In these books we will not follow a set order or system of separate precepts, which in most instances is the customary procedure in teaching any subject whatsoever, but rather, after the manner of many of the ancients, we will revive a delightful memory and repeat certain discourses on this subject which once took place among men of most unusual talents. And although I did not enter into the discourses personally, because I was in England when they were pronounced and shortly after my return learned of them from a person who faithfully narrated them to me, I shall endeavor to recall them with accuracy, in so far as memory will serve me, in order that you may know what men who are worthy of highest praise and in whose judgment unquestioning reliance can be placed in all matters have decided and believed in this matter. Nor will it be a departure from our subject to narrate the occasion of the following discourses, so that we may reach in orderly fashion the end at which our talk aims.

2. The setting of the discussion is the Ducal Palace of Urbino.

On the slopes of the Appenines almost in the center of Italy over toward the Adriatic Sea is situated the little city of Urbino, as everyone knows. Although it is among mountains, and not such pleasant ones perhaps as some others which we find in many regions, still heaven has so favored it that the countryside roundabout is very fertile and fruitful, with the result that in addition to the healthfulness of the air there is abundance of everything which supplies the requirements of human life. But among the greatest blessings which can be assigned to it, this, I believe, is the chief: that from the remote past to the present it has always been ruled by the very best lords, though in the universal misfortune of the Italian wars it too was for a while bereft of them. But without searching farther in the past we can offer good evidence of this fact in the glorious memory of Duke Federico, who in his day was the light of Italy. . . . Among his other praiseworthy works this man built on the rough terrain of Urbino a palace which is in the opinion of many the most beautiful to be found in all Italy; and he furnished it so well with every appropriate article that it appeared to be not a palace but a city in the form of a palace. And he not only furnished it with what is customarily used, such as vases of silver and hangings in richest fabrics of gold, silk, and similar materials, but by way of embellishment added to them innumerable antique statues of marble and of bronze, paintings of outstanding merit, and musical instruments of all kinds; nor did he care to have anything there unless it were very rare and excellent. Next, at very great expense he gathered together a large number of very excellent and very rare books in Greek, Latin, and Hebrew, all of which he ornamented with gold and silver, judging that this was the supreme distinction of his great palace.

3. *Guid'Ubaldo is less fortunate than his father.*

> Castiglione tells us that Federico's heir, Guid'Ubaldo, the duke at the time that the discourses in *The Courtier* are supposed to take place, was an invalid who nevertheless gathered about him a brilliant court devoted to all sorts of gentlemanly pursuits. ·

4. Castiglione describes the court of the Duchess Elisabetta Gonzaga.

All the hours of the day were apportioned among noble and pleasing exercises both of the body and of the mind; but since the Duke, owing to his infirmity, invariably went to bed very shortly after supper, everyone customarily gathered at that hour where the Duchess Elisabetta Gonzaga was. There also was always to be found Lady Emilia Pia, who, as you know, because she was endowed with such lively intelligence and judgment, seemed to be the mistress of all, while each seemed to draw good sense and worth from her. Here, then, were heard delightful discourses and inoffensive humor; and in the countenance of each person a playful gaiety was seen to be depicted, so that that house could rightly be called the true abode of merriment. And I do not think that the sweetness which springs from a beloved and cherished company was so fully tasted in any other place as it was there once upon a time; for without reckoning how greatly each of us was honored in serving a lord such as the one I have already described in an earlier place, there arose in the minds of all of us a supreme contentment every time we came into the presence of the Duchess, and it seemed that this was a chain which held all united in love, so that there was never harmony of will or heart-felt love, even among brothers, greater than that which existed there among all the men.

The same existed among the women, with whom we maintained the freest and most honorable intercourse; for every man was permitted to speak, sit, jest, and laugh with whomever he pleased; but so great was the respect which was paid to the wish of the Duchess that this very liberty was the strongest of restraints; nor was there anyone who did not consider pleasing her to be the greatest pleasure that he could possess in this world and displeasing her the greatest woe. . . .

*5. Customary pastimes of the Court of Urbino
included music, dancing, and games
of various sorts.*

But turning from this subject, I say that the custom
of all the gentlemen of the house was to betake themselves
to the Duchess immediately after supper; there, along with
other delightful entertainment, music, and dancing which
went on continuously, puzzling questions were sometimes
propounded, sometimes certain ingenious games were devised at the discretion of one or another person, in which
beneath various veils the members of the company many
times disclosed their thoughts symbolically to this or that
person, as it pleased them. Sometimes other debates arose
on various topics, or again sharp raillery was exchanged in
lively repartee; often 'devices', as we call them today, were
invented. Here then a wonderful delight was derived from
discussions of this sort, the house being filled, as I have
said, with men of noblest wit. . . .

*6. A game is to be selected for the evening
following the departure of the Pope after
his visit to Urbino in 1507.*

When Pope Julius II, by his own presence and with the
aid of the French, had reduced Bologna to obedience to the
Apostolic See in the year 1506 and was returning in the
direction of Rome, he passed through Urbino, where he was
received with all possible honor and with a magnificent and
resplendent display greater than could have been achieved
in any other noble city of Italy, barring none;* so that in
addition to the Pope, all the Cardinals and other courtiers
were thoroughly gratified; and there were some who, at-
tracted by the sweetness of that society, remained for many

---

*The Pope sojourned in Urbino from March 3 to March 7,
1507. (Translator's note).

days in Urbino after the Pope and the court had departed, during which time not only did we continue in our customary round of everyday diversions and pleasures, but each one of us endeavored to add a special something, and above all in the games, to which nearly every evening was devoted. And the procedure in these games was such that as soon as each person arrived in the presence of the Duchess he sat down, wherever he liked or where chance decreed, in a circle; and in the seating man alternated with woman, so long as any women were left there, since almost always the number of men was the greater. Thereafter they conducted themselves according to the fancy of the Duchess, who on most occasions entrusted the task to Lady Emilia. Thus, the day after the Pope's departure, when the company was assembled at the usual hour in the customary place, the Duchess desired Lady Emilia to begin the games.

7-11. Various subjects for discussion are proposed.

> The gentlemen suggest various subjects for discussion; finally it is the turn of Federico Fregoso, whose suggestion, described in the next section, finds favor.

12. It is decided that the game for the evening will be the definition of the perfect Courtier.

". . . If in any place there are men who desire to be called good Courtiers and who can judge what belongs to the perfection of Courtiership, it is reasonable to believe that they are present here. In the interest of suppressing numerous fools who, in their conceit and silliness, are persuaded that they have acquired the name of good Courtiers, I should like the evening's game to be one in which someone is selected from the company and is given the task of forming in words a perfect Courtier, explaining all the attributes and special qualities which are requisite in one who deserves that name; and on those points which are not felt appropriate every person may be permitted to enter a contradiction, as he would to someone who is conducting a disputation in the schools of philosophers."

Messer Federico was continuing with his discourse when Lady Emilia, interrupting him, said:

"If it is the Duchess's pleasure, this will be our game for the present."

The Duchess replied:

"It is my pleasure."

Thereupon nearly all the company began saying, both to the Duchess and to each other, that this was the finest game they could have played; and without waiting for each other's replies they earnestly entreated Lady Emilia to ordain who should begin it. She, turning to the Duchess, said:

"Give the order, Madame, to the one whom you would like best to assume this undertaking; for I do not wish, by selecting one person rather than another, to appear to judge which one I consider better fitted for this than the others and so do an injustice to anyone."

The Duchess replied:

"However that may be, you must make the selection yourself; and take care that your disobedience does not furnish an example to others so that they too may be wanting in obedience."

13. Ludovico da Conossa is appointed to begin the game.

Then Lady Emilia, laughing, said to Count Ludovico da Canossa: "Well, in order not to lose more time, you, Count, will be the one who will assume this undertaking after the fashion which Messer Federico has stated—not, indeed, because it seems to us that you are so good a Courtier as to know what is requisite for one, but because by your saying everything contrariwise, as we hope you will, the game will be livelier; for everyone will have something to reply to you, whereas, if someone who knew more than you had this task, he could not be contradicted in anything, since he would state the truth, and thus the game would be dull."

The Count promptly replied:

"Madame, there is no danger that one who speaks the truth will fail to be contradicted so long as you are present." And after they had laughed at his reply for a while, he continued: "But in all truth I would very willingly escape this task, as I consider it too difficult, and as I am conscious that what you have said in jest is entirely true: namely that I do not know what is fitting for a good Courtier; and I do not seek to prove this with any evidence other than the fact that from my not performing the actions one can conclude that I do not know how to perform them. . . ."

Then Lord Cesare Gonzaga said:

"Since a good part of the night has passed and many other kinds of entertainment are ready at hand, perhaps it would be well to defer this discourse until tomorrow and give the Count time to think of what he needs to say. For to discuss such a subject without preparation is a difficult thing."

The Count replied:

"I do not want to act like the man who, after having stripped to his undershirt, did not leap so far as he would have in his doublet; for I take it as a great piece of luck that the hour is so late, since I shall be forced by the shortness of the time to say little, and my not having reflected on the matter will excuse me to the extent that I shall be permitted to utter without reproach all the things that come first to my tongue." . . .

14. Should the Courtier be of noble birth?

"I desire, then, that this Courtier of ours should be noble by birth and come of a distinguished family; because failure to perform worthy actions is much less unbecoming in a man of lowly birth than in a man of high birth, who, if he strays from the path of his ancestors, stains the family name and not only wins nothing but loses what was already won. For nobility is like a clear lamp, which reveals and brings to view good works and bad and kindles and spurs to excellence as much by the fear of disgrace as by the hope of praise; and as this effulgence of nobility does not disclose the accomplishments of humble men, these lack the stimulus and the fear of that disgrace, nor do they feel thmselves bound to surpass what their ancestors have done, whereas to the noble it appears a reproach not to reach at least the mark set up for them by their forebears.

"Therefore it nearly always happens that both in arms and in other worthy actions the most distinguished men are of noble birth, because nature in each thing has implanted that secret seed which imparts a certain power and property of its origin to all that derives from it and causes all that derives from it to resemble itself. We see this not only in the breeds of horses and other animals but also in trees, the young shoots of which almost always resemble the trunk; and if in some cases they degenerate, poor cultivation is at fault. And so it happens among men, who, if they are given a good education, almost always are like those from whom they spring and often are better; but if they lack someone who tends them carefully, they become like savages and their powers never mature.

"True it is that, whether by the favor of the stars or of nature, some come into the world possessed of so many graces that it seems they were not born but some god formed them with his own hands and decked them out with all the blessings both of mind and of body; so also many are seen so silly and ill-mannered that one can only believe nature brought them into the world out of spite or mockery. Just as the latter, in most cases, are capable of producing little fruit even with unremitting application and good education, so the former attain the fulness of supreme excellence with little effort.

"But . . . I assert that between this surpassing grace and that senseless stupidity there is yet to be found a mean;

and those who are not so perfectly endowed by nature can, with study and labor, in large measure polish and correct their natural blemishes. I desire then that the Courtier should be fortunate in this respect in addition to being noble, and that he should possess by nature not only intelligence and a fine mold of figure and face, but also a certain grace and, as they say, a *blood* which makes him pleasing and attractive at first sight to anyone who sees him; and I desire that this may be an ornament which harmonizes and accompanies all his actions and which promises on the face of it that such a one is worthy of intercourse with, and favor from, every great lord.

15. The requirement of noble birth is questioned.

At this point Lord Gaspar Pallavicino, not waiting any longer, said:

"In order that our game may have the customary form and that we may not appear to value lightly the authority given us to contradict, I say that this noble birth does not seem to me so requisite in the Courtier; and if I thought I was saying something that might be new to any of us, I would adduce many men who, though born of noblest blood, have been full of vices, and on the contrary many of plebian origin who have by their worth rendered illustrious their posterity. And if what you said earlier is true, namely that there is in everything that secret power of the first seed, we should all be in the same condition, through our having had the same origin, nor would one be nobler than another. But I believe that there are many other causes for our differences and degrees of loftiness and meanness. Among them I judge Fortune to be chief, because in all worldly affairs we see her rule and seemingly make a sport of raising, often to the very skies, some favorite of hers who is without any merit whatsoever, while burying in the abyss those worthiest of being exalted. I accept entirely what you call the happiness of those that are born endowed with blessings of mind and body, but this is seen among the lowly born as well as among the nobly born, because nature does not observe these overnice distinctions. Rather, as I have said, one often sees the loftiest gifts of nature in persons of lowest station. Furthermore, since there is no acquiring this nobility either by wit or by force or by art, and since it is more often an honor paid to our ancestors than any deserved by us, I think it excessively odd to rule that, if our Courtier's parents were not noble, all his good qualities are vitiated and those other attributes that you have named do not suffice to bring him to fulness of perfection—namely beauty of face, a well-proportioned body, and that gracefulness which always makes him most pleasing to everyone at first sight."

16. The Count replies that noble birth is not essential but offers distinct advantages.

Count Ludovico then replied:

"I do not deny that even in men of humble station those very same virtues can govern that govern in men of noble birth. But in order not to repeat what we have already said or to add the many other arguments which could be adduced in praise of nobility, a thing honored always and by everyone since it is in accordance with reason that the good should spring from the good, let me say that having to shape a Courtier without any defect whatsoever and heaped with every praise, I think it necessary to make him noble, for many other reasons as well as the universal opinion which is promptly formed in favor of nobility. Let there be two courtiers who have not as yet created any impression of themselves by actions either good or bad; yet as soon as it becomes known that one was born a gentleman and the other not, the commoner will be much less esteemed by everyone than the nobleman, and he will have to expand much effort and time to impress on the minds of men the good opinion of himself which the other will have won in an instant and merely by virtue of being a gentlemen.

"And how important these impressions are everybody

can easily understand, since, speaking of our own experience, we have seen men come to this house who, although they were fools and mighty oafs, nevertheless have been reputed throughout Italy to be very great Courtiers; and although in the end they were shown up and known for what they were, still for many days they deceived us and maintained in our minds that opinion of themselves which in the beginning they had found impressed there, even though they had behaved consistently with their meagre worth. We have seen others in very low repute at the beginning, then at the end prove themselves splendidly.

"And of these mistakes there are various causes, among others the prestige of great lords who, wishing to perform miracles, sometimes proceed to bestow favor on someone who they think actually deserves the opposite. And often these lords also are deceived; but because they always have multitudes who ape them, there arises from their favor a very high reputation, with which for the most part the judgments of men fall in step; and if men discover anything contrary to the general opinion they suspect that they are deceived and always remain in expectation of something still undisclosed, because they believe that these universal opinions must somehow be founded on truth and derive from rational grounds, and also because our minds are very prone to love and to hate, as one observes at combats, games, and every other sort of contest. At these the spectators frequently become partisans of one of the sides without manifest reason, fervently desiring that their side may win and the other lose. Regarding the opinion of the characters of men, too, a good or bad reputation on first hearing inclines our mind to one of these two emotions. Thus it happens that for the most part we judge in love or in hatred. See then how great is the importance of this first impression and how hard the man who hopes to possess the rank and name of good Courtier must exert himself to make a good impression at the very beginning.

17. The Courtier's chief profession ought to be that of arms.

"But to come down to some particulars, I judge that the chief and true profession of the Courtier ought to be that of arms. Above all I desire that he exercise his profession with spirit and that he be known among other men as bold and energetic and faithful to the one he serves. And he will acquire a name for these good attributes by performing at all times and places the deeds they call for. For it is not allowable ever to fail in this without extreme reproach; and just as women's chastity, once stained, never again returns to its original state, so also the reputation of a gentleman who bears arms, if besmirched a single time in the smallest particular through cowardice or other dereliction, remains forever disgraced before the world and steeped in ignominy.

"Therefore the more accomplished our Courtier becomes in this art, the more worthy of praise he will be, although I do not consider essential to him a perfect knowledge of things, or such other attributes as are requisite for a commander. Since this subject is too vast a sea, let us be contented, as we have said, with firmness of faith, with invincible courage, and with the Courtier's being found to possess these on all occasions. For many times the courageous are recognized more in small things than in great. It is true that in serious dangers and in places where many witnesses are present we find some men who, although their heart is dead in their body, still, thrust on by shame or by the company, go forward as if with eyes shut and do their duty God knows how; yet in things which matter little and in which they think they can avoid exposing themselves to danger and nevertheless run no risk of detection, they are glad to play safe. But those who, even when they think they are not likely to be either watched, observed, or recognized by anyone, display courage and do not overlook anything, however slight, which might be a reproach to them, are possessed of that strength of mind which we seek in our Courtier.

"However, we do not care to have him make such a show of fierceness as always to be spouting bold words, to claim to have taken his cuirass as wife, and to glower with those fierce frowns which we have often seen in Berto. For what a spirited woman in the company of persons of rank said once to someone whom I do not wish to name at present can deservedly be said to men of this stamp. When in order to do him honor she invited him to dance and he refused not only to do this but also to listen to music and to take part in many other forms of entertainment that were offered him, always with the statement that frivolities of this kind were not his profession, and when finally the woman said, 'What then is your profession?' he replied with an offended look: 'Fighting'; thereupon the woman promptly said: 'I should think that now that you are not at war or on the point of fighting, it would be a good thing if you had yourself well greased and replaced in an arms-closet along with all your fighting equipment until need arises, in order not to get more rusty than you are.' And thus, amidst much laughter of the bystanders, she left him to his stupid conceit, an object of scorn. Let the man we are seeking be very bold, keen, and always in the front lines where enemies are to be found; in every other place humane, modest, restrained, shunning above all things ostentation and the shameless self-praise by which one always provokes hatred and disgust in those who hear him."

18. Shameless bragging is forbidden.

"But I," Lord Gaspar then replied, "have known few men excellent in anything whatsoever who do not praise themselves; and I think that we can very well bear with them; for when a person who knows he has merit sees that he does not achieve recognition among the unlearned through his deeds, he is resentful that his worth should lie buried

and needs must bring it to light in one way or another, in order not to be cheated of the honor which is the true reward of valiant endeavors. Therefore among the ancient writers any who is of great merit rarely refrains from praising himself. Those men are indeed intolerable who praise themselves though they are without merit, but a man of this sort we do not suppose our Courtier to be."

Then the Count said:

"If you had grasped my meaning, I condemned praising oneself shamelessly and inconsiderately, and certainly, as you say, we ought not form a bad opinion of a valorous man who praises himself modestly; however, I take that testimony as more reliable which comes from someone else's lips. I say truly that one who in praising himself does not fall into error and creates no disgust or ill will in his hearer is very circumspect indeed and in addition to the praises which he gives himself deserves those of others as well, for this feat is a most difficult one."

The Lord Gaspar said:

"This you must teach us."

The Count replied:

"Among the ancient writers there is no lack of men who have taught this; but in my opinion the whole matter consists in saying things in such a way that they do not seem to be said for that purpose but come in so apropos that one cannot refrain from uttering them; and thus while one appears always to avoid one's own praise, one utters it nevertheless—not, however, in the fashion followed by these boasters who open their mouth and let the words flow at random. As for example one of our men said a few days ago that when at Pisa he had a pike thrust clean through one thigh he thought a fly had stung him; and another declared that he used not to keep a mirror in his room because when he got angry he looked so terrifying that if he had seen his reflection he would have given himself an overpowering fright."

Everyone laughed at this, but Cesare Gonzaga rejoined:

"What are you laughing at? Do you not know that Alexander the Great, learning that it was the opinion of one philosopher that there were an infinite number of worlds, began to weep and when asked why he was weeping answered: 'Because I have conquered only one of them'—as if he had a mind to seize them all? Does this not seem greater braggadocio than the statement about the stinging of the fly?"

Then the Count said:

"Still, Alexander was a greater man than the one who said that. But men of outstanding merit should indeed be pardoned when they cherish a very high opinion of themselves; because a man who has great things to do must possess boldness to do them and confidence in himself and not be of abject or cowardly mind, yet be decidedly temperate in speech, seeming not to have so high an opinion of himself as he actually has, lest that high opinion pass over into rashness."

19. The Courtier should possess a pleasing but virile countenance.

As the Count made a slight pause here, Messer Bernardo Bibbiena said, laughing:

"I recall your saying earlier that this Courtier of ours ought to be endowed by nature with a beautifully modeled countenance and figure, along with that grace which should make him so very winning. Grace and a most beautiful countenance I think I certainly have, and for that reason it comes about that as many women as you can name burn for my love; but I am somewhat in doubt concerning the form of my body, and especially because of these legs of mine which in truth I do not find as well turned as I should wish; though I am very well satisfied with the trunk and the remainder. Describe then a little more in detail what this form of body ought to be, so that I may rid myself of this uncertainty and be left with mind at ease."

After they had laughed a while over this, the Count replied:

"Certainly grace of countenance can without falsehood be said to be yours, and I adduce no other example than this to make clear what sort of thing it is; for without doubt we see that your countenance is most agreeable and pleasing to everybody though its features are not remarkably delicate; however, it possesses a virile quality and yet is gracious, and this characteristic is found in many dissimilar types of countenance. And of such type I wish the countenance of our Courtier to be—not soft and feminine, such as many try to have who not only curl their hair and pluck their eyebrows but paint their faces in all the ways which the most loose and shameless women of the world practice; and in walking, in standing, and in every other act of theirs they seem so delicate and languid that their limbs seem ready to come apart. And they speak those words of theirs so languishingly that their spirit seems to be departing at the very instant; and the more they find themselves with men of rank, the more they indulge in this sort of deportment. Since nature has not made them women such as they apparently wish to appear and to be, they should not be looked upon as virtuous women but be driven like common prostitutes not only from the courts of great lords but from the company of gentlemen.

20. He should be of medium height and he should know how to handle all sorts of weapons.

"Coming now to the nature of his person, I call it enough that he be neither short nor tall to an extreme, because both these states evoke a certain contemptuous wonder, and men of such type are looked at almost in the way people look at monstrosities; although, if we are to offend in one or the other of the two extremes, it is less bad to be a little undersized than to exceed the reasonable measure in height; because men so enormous of body, in addition to their frequently being found dull of wit, are also unfit for any exercise of agility, a thing which I greatly desire in the Courtier. And therefore I require that he be of well-proportioned body and well-formed limbs and show strength and lightness and suppleness and know all the exercises of the body which are appropriate for a warrior.

"And among these I think the chief ought to be to handle skillfully weapons of all sorts both on foot and on horseback and to know all the advantages to be found in them and especially to have knowledge of those weapons which are ordinarily used among gentlemen. For in addition to the employment of them in warfare, in which great refinement of technique is perhaps not called for, there often occur variances between one gentleman and another from which a duel ensues, often fought with those weapons which at that moment are found at hand. Therefore knowledge of them is a great safeguard. Nor am I at all in agreement with those who say that skill is forgotten just at the moment of need; for certainly he who loses his skill in that moment gives evidence that he has first lost his courage and his wits from fear.

21. The Courtier should know how to wrestle.
conduct himself in duels, and ride.

"I believe also that it is of great importance to know how to wrestle, because wrestling is closely associated with all the weapons used in fighting on foot. Next, both for his own sake and for his friends' he ought to understand the quarrels and variances that can arise and to have a sharp eye for positions of advantage, always showing everywhere both spirit and caution. And he should not be quick to engage in these duels, except in so far as compelled by honor. For leaving out of account the great danger which the uncertain outcome involves, he who rashly and without pressing reason engages in such affairs deserves the strongest reproof, even though success be his.

"But when a man finds himself so deeply involved that

he cannot withdraw without disgrace, he must be completely resolute both in the preliminaries to the duel and in the duel itself and always display readiness and courage and not behave like some who let the matter pass off in disputes and quibbles and who, when they have the choice of weapons, select those which neither cut nor pierce and arm themselves as if they were expecting a cannonade and who, as if they were satisfied merely not to be defeated, are always on the defensive and ready to give ground to the point where they betray utter cowardice. . . .

"Arms are often employed in times of peace in various exercises, and gentlemen are seen in public shows, in the presence of the people, of gentelwomen, and of great lords. Therefore I desire that our Courtier be a consummate horseman in every type of saddle; and that besides knowing horses and the whole art of riding he devote every effort and care to advancing a little beyond the others in every point, so that he may always be recognized as outstanding among all. . . . And since it is the peculiar glory of the Italians to ride well a bridled horse, to handle horses, fiery ones especially, according to system, to run lances and to joust, let him be among the best of the Italians in this; in tourneying, holding a pass, disputing a barrier, let him be good among the best of the French; in stick throwing, running bulls, hurling spears and darts, let him be excellent among the Spanish. But above all, let him accompany every one of his movements with a certain good judgment and grace, if he wishes to merit that universal favor which is so greatly prized.

22. Certain other exercises are appropriate.

"There are also many other exercises which, while not dependent directly on arms, still have close relationship with them and greatly promote manly vigor; and among these I think that hunting is one of the chief, because it bears a certain likeness to warfare and is truly the sport for great lords and appropriate to a courtier; we know that among the ancients also it was much practiced. It is also appropriate to know how to swim, to jump, to run, to throw stones, because, besides the usefulness that may be derived from this in warfare, one often has occasion to give proof of oneself in things of this sort, from which a good name is acquired, especially among the multitude, to which one must certainly make oneself agreeable.

"Another noble exercise and one most suitable for a courtier is tennis, in which we clearly observe the formation of the body, the quickness and suppleness of each limb, and all those things which we observe in almost any other exercise. Nor do I assign a lower place to vaulting on horse, which though it be fatiguing and difficult, more than anything else makes a man very light and agile. And, besides its usefulness, if that lightness be accompanied by gracefulness, this exercise makes a finer display than any of the others.

"If then our Courtier is more than passably skillful in these exercises, I think that he ought to dispense with the others, such as turning sommersaults, rope walking, and similar things, which smack of the professional acrobat and are very little becoming to a gentleman.

"However, because one cannot continually devote oneself to these extremely fatiguing activities and because constant application produces weariness and destroys the admiration that is aroused by what is rare, we ought always to vary our existence with pursuits of different sorts. Therefore I want the Courtier to descend sometimes to more restful and calm activities and, in the interest both of avoiding unpopularity and of living on pleasant terms with everybody, to do everything the others do, of course never departing from laudable behavior and always conducting himself with that good judgment which does not let him become involved in any foolish affairs; but I wish him to laugh, chaffer, make witticisms, and dance—in such a manner, however, that he always appears sensible and circumspect and is graceful in everything he does or says."

23. Cesare Gonzaga begs leave to ask a question.

"Certainly," said Messer Cesare Gonzaga at this point, "we ought not hinder the course of this discussion; but if I kept silent I should not be doing justice to the liberty I have of speaking or to the desire to know a certain thing. And may I be forgiven for asking a question when I ought to be offering a contradiction, for I believe that this may be lawful for me after the example of Messer Bernardo, who, out of excessive anxiety to be considered a handsome man, has broken the rules of our game, by asking a question instead of offering an objection. . . .

24. How can the Courtier acquire the essential quality, grace?

"If I remember correctly, you have stated several times this evening that the Courtier should accompany his actions, his gestures, his dress—in short, his every movement, with grace; and you seem to me to use this for everything, as a seasoning without which the other qualities and good attributes are of little value. . . . But since you said that this is often a gift of nature and of the heavens and also that when grace is not entirely perfect it can with care and toil be much increased, I think that those who are born so fortunate and so rich in this treasure as some we see, have, in this respect, little need of any other teacher; for the kindly favor of heaven almost in despite of themselves leads them up higher than they aspire to go and makes them not only pleasing but astonishing in the eyes of the whole world. Therefore I am not going to discuss this gift, since it is not in our power to acquire it through our own efforts. But as to those who are endowed only just so far that they are capable of acquiring grace by exerting effort, industry, and application—I wish to know by what art, by what discipline, and by what method they can acquire grace in exercises of the body, in which you believe it to be so extremely requisite, as well as in every other thing that is done or said. Since by praising this quality so highly to us you have, I believe, raised a burning thirst in everyone to possess it, you are also, by virtue of the office imposed upon you by Lady Emilia, under obligation to quench that thirst by teaching it to us."

25. The Courtier must study under the best masters.

"I am not obligated," said the Count, "to teach you how to become gracious or anything else, but solely to show you what sort of person a perfect Courtier has to be. Nor would I ever undertake to teach you this perfection, especially since I said a little while ago that the Courtier had to know how to wrestle and to vault and to do so many other things; but I know that all are aware how well I should be able to teach you these things, never having learned them myself. It is enough that, just as a good soldier is able to tell the armorer of what style and finish and quality the gear has to be, yet does not therefore know how to teach him the way to make it or the way to hammer and temper it, so I perhaps shall be able to tell you what a perfect Courtier must be, but not to teach you how to proceed in order to become one. Nevertheless, in order to answer your question as well as it is in my power to do so, I say that, although it is almost proverbial that grace cannot be acquired by learning, the man who must learn to be graceful in bodily exercises, assuming first of all that he not incapable by nature, should begin early and learn the fundamentals from the best masters. How important Phillip, King of Macedonia, considered this matter one can understand from the fact that he wished Aristotle, so renowned a philosopher and possibly the greatest that the world has ever known, to be the one who taught the fundamentals of letters to Alexander, his son. . . .

26. He must cultivate a natural manner and shun affectation.

"Thus one who wishes to be a good disciple must not only do things well but always take all pains to make himself resemble his master and, if such a thing were possible, transform himself into him. And when he feels that he has already made some progress, he will profit greatly from observing various men of his profession and, while governing himself with that good judgment which should always guide him, go about selecting different things, now from one man, now from another. . . .

"But having on many previous occasions pondered what the source of this grace may be, leaving aside those who get it from the stars, I find a very general rule which I think has greater value in all that human beings do or say than any other rule bearing on this subject; and that is, to the full extent of one's ability, to avoid affectation as a very sharp and dangerous reef; and, to use perhaps a new term, to employ in everything a certain casualness* which conceals art and creates the impression that what is done and said is accomplished without effort and even without its being thought about. It is from this, in my opinion, that grace largely derives; for everyone appreciates the difficulty of things uncommon yet well performed, for which reason facility in these things creates the greatest admiration; and

---

*The Italian word is *sprezzatura* (literally, "disdaining"). English appears not to possess a word that conveys all that is meant by *sprezzatura*, which denotes a natural, even off-hand manner of doing things, made possible however by careful training according to the best models. *Casualness* is used in the present translation, but *nonchalance, insouciance, carelessness*, and other words have been suggested. The Italian word used to denote the opposite of *sprezzatura* is *affettazione*. Again, the English *affectation* used in this translation does not convey all that is implied concerning a studied, artificial, pretentious manner which robs one's behavior of ease and suggests lack of real acquaintance with good society. (Translator's note.)

on the other hand to strain and, as they say, 'to drag by the hair' imparts the greatest awkwardness and causes everything, no matter how important, to be held in low esteem. Therefore that may be called true art which does not appear to be art; nor ought we to devote more study to any other thing than to concealing art, for if art be disclosed, all confidence in one is destroyed and one is left in disrepute. And I recall having once read that there were certain very gifted orators among the ancients who among their other strategies endeavored to make everyone believe that they had no acquaintance whatsoever with letters, and while dissimulating their skill gave the impression that their orations were composed quite spontaneously and rather as nature and truth dictated than care and art. And had that art been detected, it would have created in the minds of the people a caution lest they be taken in by it. You see then how the betrayal of our art, together with such intent application, destroys the grace of anything whatsoever. Who among you is there who does not laugh when our Messer Pierpaulo dances after his fashion, with those little skips, legs stretched stiff to the tips of the toes, with head held motionless as if he were made all of wood, and with such concentration that it certainly seems he is counting his steps as he goes? What eye is so blind as not to see in this the ungracefulness of effort and affectation? Whereas in many men and women here present the grace of that unstudied freedom from constraint (for many call it such in bodily movements) gives the impression, by a word or laugh or easy movement, that they are not paying attention and are thinking of anything else rather than the immediate concern, so that the observer is made to believe them almost unacquainted with error or incapable of it?"

*27. However, exaggerated naturalness is itself
a form of affectation.*

Breaking in here, Messer Bernardo Bibbiena said:

"See how our Messer Roberto has at last found someone who will praise his manner of dancing, since it seems that all the rest of you make no objection. For if this excellence consists in casualness and in seeming not to pay attention and to be thinking of anything else rather than of what one is doing, then Messer Roberto has no equal in the world in dancing; for in order to persuade us thoroughly that he is not thinking of what he is doing he often lets the cloak fall from his shoulders and the slippers from his feet and dances on without picking up either."

The Count then replied:

"Seeing that you still want me to talk, I will say something also about our faults. Do you not perceive that what you call casualness in Messer Roberto is in truth affectation? For one is distinctly conscious of the fact that he tries with all diligence to seem not to pay any attention to what is happening, and this is to pay too much attention; and because it exceeds certain limits of moderation this casualness is affected and gives offense and turns out exactly the contrary of what is intended, which is to conceal art. Therefore I do not consider it less affected to let the clothes fall from one's back in being casual (which in itself is praiseworthy) than in being fastidious (which undoubtedly is in itself likewise praiseworthy) to carry one's head very still for fear of disarranging one's long locks or to keep a mirror in the crown of one's cap and a comb in one's sleeve and always have a page follow one through the streets with the sponge and the brush. For that sort of fastidiousness and that sort of casualness verge too much on the extreme, which is always offensive and opposed to that pure winning naturalness which is so pleasing to human minds. See how ungraceful a rider is when he labors to ride very rigid in the saddle and, as we are accustomed to say, 'after the Venetian manner,' in comparison with another who seems not to be thinking of the matter and who sits his horse as relaxed and secure as if he were afoot" . . .

28. Examples of naturalness and affectation
are drawn from music, painting, and speech.

Then the Lord Magnifico said:

"This can also be shown to be true in music, in which it is a grievous offense to sound two perfect consonances one after the other, such that our very sense of hearing abhors the effect and often favors a second or seventh, which in itself constitutes a harsh and unendurable dissonance. And this happens because that continuation in the perfect intervals is cloying and offers too insistent a harmony, something that is avoided by intermingling the imperfect ones to form, as it were, a contrast, so that our ears are kept more in suspense and more eagerly await and enjoy the perfect consonances, finding pleasure from time to time in that dissonance of the second or seventh as in something casually introduced."

"See then," replied the Count, "how affectation is harmful in this as in the other matters. They say, too, that it was a proverb among certain extremely fine painters of antiquity that too much industry is harmful and that Protogenes was reproached by Apelles with not knowing when to take his hands away from the picture. . . . Apelles meant to say that Protogenes did not know what was just sufficient in painting; and this was nothing else than to reproach him for being affected in his work.

"Besides being the true source from which grace arises, the virtue which is the contrary of affectation and which for the moment we are calling casualness entails a further garnishment, which, in accompanying any human action whatsoever, however inconsequential, not only quickly reveals the knowledge of the man who performs the action but often causes us to think his knowledge much greater than it is in reality. For it implants in the minds of the spectators the notion that one who so easily does well knows how to do much more than what he is doing, and if he expended study and labor on what he is doing he could do it much better. And to use again the same examples, notice that if a man who is handling arms, whether he be casting a spear or holding a sword or other weapon in his hand, without taking thought places himself lightly in an attitude of readiness, with such ease that his body and all his limbs seem to fall into that posture naturally and without any effort, he persuades everybody that he has absolute mastery in that exercise even when he does nothing further. Likewise, in dancing a single step, a solitary graceful and effortless movement of the body quickly reveals the proficiency of the dancer. A musician who in singing produces a single tone terminating with agreeable intonation in a double acciaccatura and produces it with such ease that he seems to have done so unconsciously, through that single feat lets it be known that his skill extends much beyond what he is displaying. Often in painting, too, a single unlabored line, a single stroke of the brush executed with ease in such manner that the hand seems to move of itself to its proper aim according to the painter's intention, undirected by effort or any art at all, reveals clearly the skill of the workman, though thereafter each person may express his opinion of the worth of the skill as his judgment dictates; and the same thing happens in everything else.

"Thus our Courtier will be considered excellent and in all things will have grace, especially in speaking, if he shuns affectation. Into this error many men fall, and sometimes more than any others certain of our Lombards, who if they have been a single year away from home, upon their return begin at once to speak the Roman dialect and sometimes Spanish or French, and God knows how. And all this proceeds from too eager a desire to show that one knows a great deal, and in this fashion one expends study and hard work to acquire a very repulsive fault. For indeed I would impose on myself no light task if in these discourses of ours I were minded to employ those ancient Tuscan words which long since have been eliminated from the usage of present-day Tuscans; and after all that trouble I believe everybody would laugh at me."

29. The Count rejects the suggestion that archaisms lend beauty to writing.

Then Messer Federico said:

"Truly, in conversing among ourselves, as we are now doing, those ancient Tuscan words might be objectionable, because, as you point out, they might place a strain on both the speaker and the hearer, and many would understand them only with difficulty. But a writer, I seriously believe, would make a mistake not to use them, because they lend much grace and authority to the writings and because there arises from them a language graver and more freighted with majesty than from words in current use."

"I do not know," replied the Count, "what grace or authority can be conferred on writing by those words which ought to be avoided not only in the mode of speaking which we are using at present (as you yourself confess) but also in any other which can be imagined. For if any man of good judgment, whosoever he be, has occasion to deliver a speech about weighty matters in the very senate of Florence, the chief city of Tuscany; or even to speak privately with a person of rank in that city about important business; or to talk with a very intimate friend about matters of pleasure or with women or with men about love: whether he be engaged in jesting and merriment at entertainments or at games —indeed wherever it may be and whatever may be the time, the place, or the subject—I am sure that he would be on his guard against using those old Tuscan words. And if he did use them, besides making a fool of himself he would give not a little pain to everyone who listened to him.

"Therefore I think it a very strange thing to employ those words as sound in writing which are avoided as objectionable in every manner of speaking and to propose that something which is never excusable in speaking should be the most suitable style one could use in writing. For indeed in my opinion, writing is nothing other than a form of speech which remains even after one has finished speaking —it is something like a reflection or, more exactly, the continued life of the spoken words. And therefore in speech, which is dissipated the instant the voice is uttered, certain things are perhaps acceptable which are not so in writing, because writing preserves the words and submits them to the judgment of the reader and allows him time to give them mature consideration. And therefore it is reasonable that greater application be devoted to making writing more cultivated and correct, not however in order that the written words should be unlike the spoken, but that in writing one should choose from the finest words that are used in speaking. And if in writing that were permissible which is not permissible in speaking, there would in my opinion result from this a very grave impropriety; namely, that greater liberties might be taken where greater care is needed, and the effort that is expended on writing would harm instead of helping. Moreover, this is certain: what is proper in writing is proper also in speaking, and that speech is finest which resembles fine writing. I believe also that to be understood is much more requisite in writing than in speaking. . . . Therefore I should recommend that besides avoiding many old Tuscan words one also acquire in both writing and speaking a command of those words which are today in common use in Tuscany and in the other regions of Italy and which possess some beauty of sound. And I think that anyone who binds himself to any other law is not entirely certain of not falling into that much-censured affectation of which we were speaking earlier."

30. Federico Fregoso maintains a contrary opinion.

Then Messer Federico said:
"My Lord Count, I cannot gainsay your claim that writing is a mode of speaking. Indeed, I say that if the words

that are spoken contain in themselves any obscurity, the discourse does not penetrate the mind of the hearer and in passing away without being understood comes to nothing. This does not happen in writing; for if the words a writer uses involve a small amount, I will not say of difficulty, but of subtlety hidden away and therefore not so readily caught as the sort of thing conveyed by words used in everyday conversation, they confer a kind of enhanced authority on the writing and cause the reader to go more warily and ponder more thoroughly and find delight in the wit and learning of the writer; and after exerting himself a little in exercising good judgment, the reader tastes the pleasure to be found in achieving things difficult. And if the ignorance of the reader is so great that he cannot overcome these difficulties, no blame attaches to the writer, nor on this account should his language be held to lack beauty.

Furthermore, I believe that in writing it is proper to use those Tuscan words that were used only by the Tuscans of old because using them is strong testimony, confirmed by time, that they are good words and adequately convey the idea for which they are used. And besides this they possess that favor and respect which antiquity confers not only on words but on buildings, on statues, on paintings, and on all things of which enough remains to perpetuate the past; and frequently solely by their splendor and distinction they give beauty to style, by whose force and elegance any subject, however humble, can be so adorned that it deserves highest commendation.

"On the other hand this current usage of yours by which you set so much store seems very dangerous to me and often can be noxious; and if some incorrect practice in speech is found to be prevalent in many illiterate people, I do not think it ought for that reason to be taken as a rule and be copied by others. Besides this, the usages are extremely various, nor is there any important city in Italy which does not have a fashion of speaking different from that of all the others; however, since you do not feel constrained to declare which fashion is the best, a man could adopt the Bergamask just as well as the Florentine, and according to you he would commit no error. I think then that anyone who wishes to avoid all uncertainty and to feel quite assured must necessarily resolve to imitate a figure who is regarded as sound by agreement of all and always take him as guide and shield against such as have a mind to carp. And this figure (among writers in the vernacular I mean) I think ought to be no other than Petrarch and Boccaccio; and the man who departs from these two gropes along like one who walks in darkness without a light and thus often misses the road. But we men of today are so rash that we do not condescend to do what the good men of antiquity did; namely, we do not devote ourselves to imitation, without which I think no one can write well. And I believe that strong evidence for this is provided by Virgil, who, although he robbed all later men of the hope that any could ever imitate him well, wished himself to imitate Homer."

31. Giuliano de' Medici states his opinion on this subject.

> The question concerning the use of old Tuscan words is referred to the Magnifico Giuliano de' Medici, as a Tuscan and a Florentine. He tells them that he avoids Tuscan words not in current use.

32. The Duchess directs the Count to continue the exposition of his views on speech and writing.

Then the Duchess said:

"Let us not depart from our original subject and let us allow Count Ludovico to teach the Courtier how to speak and to write well, whether it be Tuscan or what you will."

The Count replied:

"I have already said what I know about the subject, and I believe the same rules that serve to teach us the one also serve to teach the other. But since you command me to do it, I will say in reply to Messer Federico what occurs to me, his opinion being different from mine. . . .

33. What is essential is sound thought and well-planned expression.

"As for myself, I would, then, always avoid using these old words, except in certain situations, and in these situations still very rarely; and I think that people who use them in any other way are as mistaken as a man who should want to live on acorns still in order to imitate the ancients, although there was plenty of corn to be had. And because you say that outmoded words solely by the luster of antiquity so greatly enhance every subject, however humble, that they have the power to render it worthy of high praise, I reply that I do not set so much store either by these old words or even by those in good standing that I judge it reasonable to prize them unless they contain the sap of fine thoughts. For the separation of thoughts from words is a separation of soul from body, something that cannot be done in either instance without destruction. Therefore what chiefly matters and is needful for the Courtier in order that he may speak and write well is, I think, knowledge, because one who knows nothing and who does not have anything in his mind that merits being understood is powerless to say or write anything. Next, he should arrange in good order what he has to say or write; then express it well in words which, if I am not mistaken, ought to be proper, carefully chosen, striking, suitably ordered, and above all in use by the general populace; for it is these very ones which create the nobility and magnificence of the discourse if the speaker possesses good judgment and application and knows how to select the most accurate terms for what he wishes to say, how to heighten their effect, and how, by molding them like wax to his will, to set them out in such place and with such order that at first glance they reveal and proclaim their nobility and glory like paintings placed in good and proper light.

"And this I say about writing as well as about speaking, for which however certain things are requisite which are not necessary in writing, such as a good voice, not too weak or too soft like a woman's nor yet too harsh and too rough like a rustic's, but sonorous, clear, smooth, and well modulated, with ready utterance and suitable manners and gestures, which in my opinion consist in certain movements of the whole body, not exaggerated or violent but restrained, with composed features and a play of the eyes that lends grace, harmonizes with the words, and as much as possible conveys in conjunction with the gestures the meaning and feeling of the speaker. But all these things will be fruitless and of little significance if the thoughts expressed by the words are not striking, ingenious, penetrating, choice, and weighty, according to the need."

34 to 39. The Count sets forth his doctrines of usage and imitation in language.

In Sections 34 through 39 Count Ludovico continues his remarks on useage, giving the Courtier freedom to use any words that are in good standing, whatever their source; to employ existing words in new senses; and to introduce new words derived with discrimination from words in Latin. In Section 35 the Count sums up his position, as follows:

"Thus good usage in speech originates. I believe, with men of intelligence who have developed good judgment through learning and experience and in the light of it concur and agree in accepting the words they consider good, which are recognized not by method or rule of any sort, but by intuitive judgment."

He agrees with the Magnifico that if Petrarch and Boccaccio were then alive they would reject many words that appear in their writings. As to imitation of models, the Count reasons that the greatest writers of antiquity did not imitate slavishly but, like artists of his day, developed their own style as their genius dictated. Slavish or forced imitation hampers or destroys natural genius. Federico Fregoso offers objections, but Emilia puts an end to the digression by commanding the Count to take up the subject of the Courtier where he left off.

41. The Courtier must be a man of virtue and integrity.

You can appreciate how contrary and fatal affectation is to the grace of every function not only of the body, but likewise of the mind, concerning which we have as yet said little, though we should not therefore pass it over. For as the mind is much more noble than the body, so also it deserves to be more cultivated and enriched. And as to how this should be accomplished in our Courtier, let us leave aside the precepts of so many wise philosophers who write on this subject and define the powers of the mind and so subtly dispute about their worth, and let us, keeping to our subject, say in few words that it is enough he should be, as they say, a man of virtue and integrity; for in this are comprehended the practical wisdom, justice, fortitude, and temperance of mind and all the other qualities which attend upon so honored a name. And I feel that he alone is the true moral philosopher who wishes to be good; and for that purpose he needs few precepts other than that wish. . . .

42-44. Next in importance to virtue comes knowledge of humane letters.

"But with the exception of goodness, the true and chief ornament of the mind in each of us is, I think, letters. . . . I desire that in letters [our Courtier] should be more than passably learned, at least in these studies which men call humanities, and that he be acquainted not only with Latin but also with Greek, for the sake of the numerous and varied works which have been superbly written in that language. Let him be versed in the poets, and no less in the orators and historians. Let him also be trained in the writing of verse and prose, especially in our vernacular tongue. For in addition to the private enjoyment which he will derive, he will, thanks to this, never find himself at a loss for pleasing pastime with women, who for the most part love such things.

"And if, either because of other employment or because of lack of study he does not arrive at such perfection that his compositions are worthy of much praise, let him take the precaution of concealing them in order not to make others laugh at him and let him show them only to a friend whom he can trust, because they will benefit him to this extent at least that through that training he will know how to judge the works of others, for indeed it rarely happens that a person not accustomed to writing, however learned he be, can ever fully appreciate the labor and ingenuity of writers or enjoy the sweetness and excellence of styles and those latent niceties which are often found in the ancients. And besides that, these studies make him fluent and, as Aristippus replied to that tyrant, bold enough to speak with confidence to everyone. I greatly desire furthermore that our Courtier hold fixed in his mind one precept, namely, that in this and in every other thing he always be attentive and cautious rather than daring, and that he guard against persuading himself mistakenly that he knows what he does not know; for we are all by nature much more eager for praise than we should be, and our ears love the melody of the words which sing our praises more than any other song or sound, however sweet; and yet often, like the Siren's voices, these words bring shipwreck to any man who does not stop his ears against music so deceiving. Recognizing this danger, some among the sages of antiquity have written books telling us how we may distinguish the true friend from the flatterer. But what benefit has come of this if many, nay innumerable, are those who clearly realize that they are being flattered and yet love the flatterer and loathe the man who tells them the truth? And often it appears to them that the man who praises is too niggardly in what he says; so they themselves come to his aid and say such things about themselves as make the most shameless flatterer blush.

"Let us leave these blind men in their error and see to it that our Courtier is so sound of judgment that he cannot be made to take black for white or think highly of himself except in such measure as he clearly knows to be just. . . . On the contrary, in order not to err, even if he knows very well that the praises that are given him are just, let him not concur in them too openly or confirm them without some show of opposition, but rather let him modestly come near to denying them, always claiming and actually considering arms as his chief calling and all the other good attributes as ornaments of them. Let him observe this caution especially among soldiers, in order not to behave like those who in their studies wish to appear men of war and among men of war wish to appear men of letters. In this fashion and for the reasons which we have given, he will avoid affectation, and even the commonplace things that he does will appear very impressive."

45. Bembo objects that letters rather than arms ought to be the Courtier's chief glory.

At this point Messer Pietro Bembo said in reply:

"I do not know, Count, why you should desire that this Courtier, accomplished in letters and possessed of so many other qualities, should consider everything an ornament of arms and not arms and the rest an ornament of letters, which in and for themselves are as much superior to arms in worth as the mind is to the body, since the pursuit of letters belongs properly to the mind, as that of arms does to the body."

The Count then replied:

"Rather, the pursuit of arms belongs to the mind and to the body. But I am not desirous of having you, Messer Pietro, as judge of this dispute, because you would be too suspect of bias in the eyes of one of the parties; and since this debate has long been carried on by the most learned men, there is no need to renew it. However, I consider it settled in favor of arms and I stipulate that our Courtier, since I can shape him according to my will, shall also consider the matter so. And if you are of contrary opinion, wait until you hear of a dispute over it in which those who defend the case for arms may as lawfully use arms as those who defend letters use those same letters in their defence. For if each can avail himself of his own instruments, you will see that the men of letters will lose. . . .

47. The Courtier should be an accomplished musician.

"My lords . . . , you must know that I am not satisfied with the Courtier if he is not also a musician and if besides understanding music and reading notes readily he does not know a variety of instruments; for if we consider the matter carefully, we can find no repose from toil or medicine for ailing minds more wholesome and commendable for leisure time than this; and especially at courts, where much is done not only to provide the relief from vexations that music offers all of us but also to please the women, whose delicate and impressionable spirits are easily penetrated by harmony and filled with sweetness. Therefore it is no wonder if in ancient and in modern times women have always been favorably disposed toward musicians and have found music a most welcome food for the spirit."

Thereupon Lord Gaspar said:

"Music, along with many other follies, I consider suitable indeed for women and perhaps also for some who possess the appearance of men, but not for those who truly are men and who ought not to unman their minds with pleasures and thus incline them to be afraid of death."

"Do not say such a thing," answered the Count; "for I will here set forth on a vast sea of praise of music, and I will recall to what a degree among the ancients it was always extolled and regarded as something holy and how widely the wisest philosophers held that the world is fashioned of music and that the heavens produce harmony as they move and, moreover, that our soul was formed according to the same principles and therefore awakens and, as it were, quickens its powers through music. For this reason it is recorded that Alexander was so warmly aroused by it on a certain occasion that almost against his will he was obliged to rise from the banquet and rush to arms; then, as the musician altered the quality of the tone, to grow mild and return from arms to banqueting . . .

"Have you not read that music was one of the first disciplines that the good old Chiron taught Achilles, when Achilles, whom he reared from the time of milk and cradle, was at a tender age; and the wise master desired that the hands which were to spill so much Trojan blood should be often busied with the music of the cithara? What soldier, pray, will there be who is ashamed to imitate Achilles, not to mention many other famous commanders whom I could name? Therefore do not be disposed to deprive our Courtier of music, which not only softens the minds of men but often makes the fierce become gentle; and one can be certain that if a man does not enjoy music his spirits are all out of tune."

48. Giuliano de' Medici wishes to know how the Courtier is to apply his attributes in actual practice.

Since the Count was silent for a little while at this point, the Magnifico Giuliano said:

"I am not at all of Lord Gaspar's opinion; on the contrary I believe, for the reasons that you state and for many others, that music is not only an ornament but a necessity for the Courtier. I should greatly like you to declare in what way this and the other attributes which you assign to him are to be put into practice, both at what time and after what fashion. For many things which in themselves deserve praise frequently become highly unsuitable when done at the wrong time. And by way of contrast, some things which appear of small weight are much valued when they are properly managed."

49. Before answering Giuliano the Count
recommends that the Courtier be taught to
draw and to understand painting.

Then the Count said:

"Before we enter into this subject I want to talk of another matter which, since I consider it of great importance, should, I think, by no means be left out by our Courtier. And this is knowing how to draw and possessing an understanding of the true art of painting. Do not marvel if I desire this skill which today perhaps is judged to be a craft and little fitting for a gentleman; for I recall having read that the ancients, especially through the whole of Greece, used to require that children of noblemen give attention to painting in school, as something wholesome and requisite; and that this subject was admitted into the first rank of the liberal arts and subsequently by public edict was forbidden to be taught to slaves. Among the Romans also it was held in the highest honor. . . .

"And to tell the truth I think that anyone who does not value this art is very much a stranger to reason; for the universe in its structure, with the wide heaven of bright stars surrounding it and in the middle the earth girdled by the seas, figured with mountains, valleys, and rivers, and embellished by trees of many different kinds and by lovely flowers and plants, one can call a noble and magnificent picture executed by the hand of nature and of God; and the man who can imitate it I consider worthy of great praise; nor can one succeed in this without the knowledge of many things, as anyone who tries it well knows.

"Therefore the ancients held both art and artist in highest esteem, for which reason art arrived at the peak of all excellence. And quite decisive evidence of this fact can be drawn from the ancient statues of marble and bronze which are still to be seen. And although painting is different from sculpture, still both of them spring from one and the same source, and that is good drawing. Furthermore, just as the statues of the ancients are superlative, so also one may believe their paintings were, and so much the more in the measure that paintings are susceptible of higher technique."

50. Joanni Cristoforo Romano asserts that sculpture is a higher art than painting.

Then Lady Emilia, turning to Joanni Cristoforo Romano, who was seated there with the others, said:

"What do you think of this idea? Will you agree that painting is susceptible of higher technique than sculpture?

Joanni Cristoforo replied:

"Madame, it is my belief that sculpture involves greater labor, art, and worth than painting."

The count replied:

"Because statues are more lasting, one might say that they are of greater worth. For when they are created to preserve a record of the past, they fulfill better the purpose for which they are created than painting does. But in addition to serving as records both painting and sculpture are created for ornament also; and for this purpose painting is much superior. If painting is not so diuturnal, so to speak, as sculpture is, still it is very long-lived; and as long as it lasts it is much more pleasing."

Then Joanni Cristofor replied:

"Truly, I think that you speak contrary to what you really believe; and you are doing it all in deference to your friend Rafaello. Perhaps also you feel that the excellence in painting which you recognize in him is so supreme that sculpture cannot attain that height; but reflect that this is a matter of praise due to an artist, not to the art."

Then he added:

"And it seems clear to me that both of them are imitation of nature by art; but I really do not see how you can say that the truth and that essential character which nature imparts are not more closely imitated in a figure of marble or of bronze, in which the members are all rounded, molded, and dimensioned as nature makes them, than in a painting, in which one sees nothing more than the surfaces and those pigments which deceive the eyes; and surely you will not tell me that *being* is not closer to truth than *seeming*. I also believe that sculpture is more difficult, for if an error is made in it you cannot make a correction, since the marble does not unite again, and you must begin on a new figure—something which does not happen in painting, for one can make changes, adding here and taking away there, always improving things."

51. The Count prefers painting because it can imitate nature more fully than sculpture can.

The Count said, laughing:

"I do not speak in deference to Rafaello, and you must not by any means account me so unlearned that I do not appreciate the excellence of Michel 'Angelo and of you yourself and of others in sculpture; but I am speaking of the art and not of the artists. And you do indeed say rightly that both arts are imitation of nature; but it is not entirely true that painting *seems* and sculpture *is*. For, though statues are all in the round like the living creature, and painting is seen only on surfaces, many things are wanting in statues but not in painting, and above all lights and shadows. For flesh gives off one light and marble another, and the painter imitates this effect according to nature with various degrees of light and dark, according to need, something that the sculptor cannot do. And if indeed the painter does not make the figure in the round, he shows the muscles and members rounded in such a way that they would join those parts which are not seen, contriving it so we can well perceive that the painter is cognizant of the unseen parts and directs his thought to them.

"And this calls for another, even more demanding, technique in order to depict those members that are foreshortened and that grow smaller in proportion to the distance according to the principle of perspective, which by the effect of proportional lines, of colors, of lights and shadows, makes us see even on a surface of vertical wall the horizontal plane and the far distance in whatever dimensions the painter pleases. Then do you think the imitation of the natural colors in reproducing flesh, fabrics, and all other colored objects is of little significance? The sculptor cannot begin to do this. Neither can he express the gracious look of black eyes and blue ones, with the radiance of those amorous rays. He cannot show the color of yellow hair, or the refulgence of armor and weapons, or a dark night, or a storm at sea, or flashes and bolts of lightning, or the burning of a city, or the coming of the rose-colored dawn with its rays of gold and purple. In short, he cannot show sky, sea, earth, mountains, woods, fields, gardens, rivers, cities or houses; but the painter can do all that.

52. The knowledge of painting develops connoisseurship in art and a deeper appreciation of human beauty.

"For this reason I think painting nobler and susceptible of higher technique than sculpture and I think that in the hands of the ancients it was of supreme excellence, as was everything else, a fact still recognized by means of some small remains that survive, especially in the grottos of Rome, but much more clearly through the writings of the ancients, in which such honorable and frequent mention is made both of the works and of the masters; and through them we grasp how highly these men were always honored by great lords and by commonwealths. . . .

"Therefore let it be enough simply to say that it is also fitting for our Courtier to have a knowledge of painting, since it is whloesome and useful and was prized in those times when men were of much greater worth than they are now. And even when no utility or pleasure is ever derived from it other than that it aids in knowing how to judge the excellence of ancient and modern statues, of vases, of buildings, of medals, cameos, intaglios, and similar things, still it makes us recognize the beauty of living bodies, not only in the refinement of countenance but also in the proportions of all the rest, in men as in every other animal. Behold then how knowledge of painting is the source of a very great pleasure; and let those men take note of this who are so happy contemplating the beauties of women that they think themselves in paradise yet do not know how to paint; if they knew how to do it they would have even more enjoyment, because they would grasp more completely that beauty which engenders in their heart so much contentment.

53-56. Giuliano de' Medici's question is proposed as the topic for the next evening's meeting.

Since the hour is late the company agrees to postpone to the next evening the discussion of the subject proposed by Giuliano de' Medici, which was the way in which the Courtier is to display his qualities and accomplishments in particular times, places, and pursuits.

How the Attributes of the Courtier Are to Be Applied on Particular Occasions

In Book Two Federico Fregoso is the principal speaker. We are told that in specific situations the Courtier is to be governed by the precepts stated by Ludovico da Canossa in Book I: that he should use good sense in every action, that he should avoid affectation, that in what he is doing or saying he should take into consideration the place, the company, the motive, his age, profession, and aim, and the means of accomplishing his aim. In Book Two, Federico applies these precepts in the following ways: The courtier will not risk his life for trifles and for mere applause, but only for worthy objects and for the sake of honor; he will be suitably equipped and dressed and the devices on his banners will be appropriate and ingenious. He will not display his talent before audiences of rustics or enter into direct competition with rustics in wrestling or other contests. He will always preserve a certain dignity in public. He will never dance lively dances except in private, but if he is masked or disguised he may dance them in public even though his identity is known.

In music the courtier should be skilled, but he should seem to consider music a mere pastime. Singing and playing stringed and keyed instruments befit the Courtier. He should avoid performance before the common crowd. An old man should play and sing only in private and for his own pleasure, since most songs are love songs and performing them in public makes an old man look ridiculous.

In conversation with his prince, the Courtier should aim at pleasing his prince, never appearing vexed, melancholy, or taciturn and never flattering, lying, boasting, or begging favors for himself.

The Courtier's clothes should be appropriate to the occasion, whatever the style; they should be of black or some dark color for ordinary occasions and of cheerful colors if they are to be worn over armor. They should be elaborate and showy for public ceremonies, festivals, masquerades, and the like.

Dress, choice of friends, the games he plays, his table manners—all help to produce first impressions of the Courtier, which are so important in determining the esteem in which he is held. In everything the Courtier should exercise good judgment and avoid offensive and boorish conduct. Even in humorous talk the Courtier must exercise control over his wit by using it discreetly. Some amusing talk is fitting and some not fitting for the Courtier.

Bernardo Bibbiena is assigned the task of describing the nature of humor and the types of verbal humor, and he and the others supply examples. There are, according to Bibbiena, three types of humor: amusing stories, brief witty sayings, and practical jokes. The Courtier may practice all three types, but with discretion. He is not to jeer at misfortune, make jokes about serious offenses that deserve punishment, or treat sacred things lightly and blasphemously. Especially, he must not say salacious things before women or make jokes that reflect on a woman's honor.

Gaspar Pallavicino objects to the reservations regarding women, claiming that women even more than men like indecent stories, though women pretend not to. The discussion of this point leads to the appointment of the Magnifico Giuliano de' Medici to describe the ideal Court Lady at the next evening's meeting.

BOOK THREE

The Attributes of the Court Lady and the Character of Women in General

The Court Lady as described by the Magnifico is to possess the same virtues as the Courtier and undergo the same training in letters, music, painting, dancing and other graces; also she should avoid affectation and cultivate *sprezzatura*. She is to avoid manly exercises and manners and preserve a feminine sweetness and delicacy. For example, she should not play on drums or trumpets, or take part in tennis or hunting. Above all she should acquire a pleasant affability in entertaining men, being neither too bashful nor too bold in company.

Gaspar Pallavicino declares such a woman impossible; women are imperfect creatures. The Magnifico answers this with the proposition that since two members of the same species have the same essential substance, one cannot be essentially less perfect than the other. Pallavicino counters with the claim that man is to woman as form is to matter; woman is imperfect without man. The argument follows these metaphysical lines for a while; then the Magnifico undertakes to show that for every great man there are equally admirable women to be cited, both in ancient and in modern times.

Lord Gaspar Pallavicino continues to insist that women are chaste only through fear of punishment. Cesare Gonzaga then takes up the defense of women, citing cases of women who defended their chastity to the death and describing the wiles which men use to overcome female chastity; then, passing on to the Courtly Love tradition, he asserts that all the refinements of life are cultivated in order to please women.

Finally the discussion turns to the way the Court Lady should respond to talk of love. The Magnifico's opinion is that only unmarried women should allow themselves to fall in love, and then only when love is likely to end in marriage. All physical gratification outside marriage is forbidden. Federico Fregoso suggests that where there is no possibility of divorce a woman whose husband hates her should be permitted to bestow her love elsewhere. The Magnifico replies that she may bestow only spiritual love. Pallavicino denounces women because they love to drive a lover mad by refusing their favors for a very long while and then, when the lover's appetite is dulled by exasperation, at last bestowing favors that can no longer be fully enjoyed by him.

Ottaviano Fregoso expresses some regret that the contention over women has prevented discussion of other attributes of the Courtier. The Duchess desires him to present his ideas on the subject, but because the hour is late the discourse is postponed until the next night and is presented in the first part of Book Four.

BOOK FOUR

How the Courtier Should Serve His Prince and How the Courtier Should Conduct Himself in Love

1-2. Castiglione records subsequent fortunes and misfortunes of several speakers in the dialogues.

> In the first two sections of Book IV Castiglione laments the deaths of three speakers in *The Courtier* who died not long after the discussions took place: Gaspar Pallavicino, Cesare Gonzaga, and Roberto da Bari. Castiglione also tells us that other speakers have attained positions of importance in church and state, as can be seen from the list printed at the beginning of this translation.

3. The Duchess commands that the discussions be resumed.

It appears . . . from what Lord Gaspar Pallavicino used to tell, that on the following day, after the discourses contained in the preceding Book, little was seen of Lord Ottaviano. On that account many were of the opinion that he had withdrawn so that he could without hindrance think out carefully what he had to say. Therefore, when the company had rejoined the Duchess at the customary hour, it was necessary to make a diligent search for Lord Ottaviano, who did not appear for some time, so that many lords and ladies of the court began to dance and to give their attention to other pleasures, with the idea that for that evening there would be no more discourse about the Courtier. And everyone was already busy, one with one thing and another with another, when Lord Ottaviano arrived almost when he was no longer expected. And seeing that Messer Cesare Gonzaga and Lord Gaspar were dancing, he said, laughing, after making a bow to the Duchess:

"I quite expected to hear Lord Gaspar say something ill of the ladies again this evening; but now that I see him dancing with one, I think that he has made peace with them all, and I am happy that the dispute or, to term it more correctly, the discourse of the Courtier, is concluded."

"It is not concluded as yet," answered the Duchess, "because I am not so much the enemy of the men as you are of the women; and therefore I do not wish the Courtier to be defrauded of any part of the honor due him and of those adornments that you yourself promised him last evening."

And speaking thus she commanded that when that dance was over they should all seat themselves in the customary way, which they did; and while all sat with great attention, Lord Ottaviano said. . . :

4. Courtiership is not an end in itself.

". . . Continuing the discourse of these lords, which I approve and endorse in its entirety, I say that among things that we call good there are some which by nature and in themselves are always good, such as temperance, fortitude, health, and all the virtues which bring us peace of mind; others which are good by virtue of various relationships and by virtue of the end toward which they are directed, such as the laws, liberty, riches, and comparable things. I think therefore that the perfect Courtier of the kind which Count Ludovico and Messer Federico have described can be truly a good thing and worthy of praise—not however by nature or in himself but relative to the end to which he can be directed. For in truth, if in being noble, graceful, and charming and skilled in so many exercises, the Courtier produces no other fruit than to be such as he is for his own sake, I would not consider that to possess this perfection of Courtiership a man would be justified in expending so much study and toil as the acquisition of it demands. On the contrary, I would say that many of those accomplishments which are assigned to him, such as dancing, revelling, singing and playing, were frivolities and vanities and in a man of rank worthy of censure rather than of praise. For this refinement in dress, these devices, these witticisms, and other things of the sort which belong to dalliance with women and to love affairs, even though many other people think the opposite, often only make minds effeminate and corrupt youth and lead it to the most lascivious way of living, from which afterwards stem the consequences that the name *Italian* is brought into reproach and only a few men are found who dare, I do not say to die, but even to expose themselves to danger. And certainly there are numberless other things which, if labor and attention were devoted to them, would give birth to much greater usefulness both in peace and in war than any such Courtiership as this taken by itself.

"But if these activities of the Courtier are directed toward that good end to which they ought to be and which I have in mind, I truly think them neither dangerous nor futile, but extremely useful and deserving of infinite commendation.

5. The end of Courtiership is the exercising of beneficial influence over the prince.

"Now in my estimation the end of the perfect Courtier, which has not been discussed up to this point, is to win for himself by means of the traits ascribed to him by these lords the good will and mind of the prince whom he serves, to such a point that this Courtier, without fear or danger of displeasing the prince, can tell and always does tell him the truth concerning everything proper for him to know. And if the Courtier knows that the prince's mind is bent on doing something unbecoming, he may dare to oppose the prince and in a courteous way take advantage of the favor acquired through his good traits to draw the prince away from every evil design and lead him into the path of virtue. And thus, by possessing goodness in himself such as these lords have ascribed to him, accompanied by readiness of wit and charm and by practical wisdom and acquaintance with letters and so many other things, the Courtier will in every instance be able adroitly to show his prince how much honor and usefulness must come to him and his people from justice, from liberality, from magnanimity, from mildness, and from all the other virtues which befit a good prince; and, contrarily, how much infamy and injury arise from the opposite vices. Therefore I believe that, just as music, revels, games, and other pleasurable activities are, so to speak, the flower of Courtiership, so to draw or assist the prince to the good and to frighten him from the bad are its true fruit.

"And since the worth of doing good consists above all in two things, one of which is to choose for ourselves an end toward which our intent is pointed and which should be truly good, the other to know how to find out fitting means and acts to lead us to the proposed end, it is certain that the mind of the man who intends to bring it about that his prince is not deceived by anyone, that he does not give ear to flatterers or to slanderers and liars, and that he knows good and evil and loves the one and loathes the other is aiming at the highest end.

6. *Flatterers encourage ignorance and conceit in princes.*

"I think further that the traits ascribed to the Courtier by these lords can constitute a good means for arriving at that end. And this is so because the greatest among the numerous failings which we see today in many of our princes are ignorance and conceit; and the root of these two evils is nothing other than lying, a vice which is deservedly hateful both to God and to men and more hurtful to princes than to anyone else; for princes have the greatest dearth of the very thing of which they ought to have the greatest abundance—that is, of the sort of man who will tell them the truth and put them in mind of the good. The reason is that the enemies of princes are not moved by love to perform these duties, but on the contrary are glad when princes live wickedly and never amend; on the other hand these enemies dare not openly rebuke princes through fear of being punished. Furthermore, the friends who have ready access to them are few, and those few hesitate to take princes to task for their failings as freely as they do private persons; and often, in order to win grace and favor they devote themselves to nothing else but suggesting things that delight and tickle the mind of princes, even when these things are evil and unclean; so that they are changed from friends into flatterers and in order to derive usefulness from that intimate relationship they speak and act always with compliance, and for the most part make their way by lies which engender in the mind of the prince an ignorance not only of things around him but also of himself; and this can be called the greatest and most monstrous lie of all because the ignorant mind is self-deceived and lies inwardly to itself.

7. The effect of injustice and tyranny in princes is described.

"From this it comes that lords . . . pass from ignorance to extreme conceit, such that thereafter they do not admit counsel or opinion of others; and because they believe that knowing how to rule is an easy thing and that to succeed in it requires no other art or training except force alone, they turn their mind and all their thoughts to preserving the power they possess, thinking that true happiness lies in being able to do what we please.

"Hence some loathe reason and justice, thinking that justice, should they be disposed to follow it, would inevitably be a check upon them and constitute a course that could reduce them to dependence and lessen for them the felicity and pleasure which they find in ruling; and that their authority would not be perfect and whole if they were constrained to obey duty and righteousness, because they think that the man who obeys is not truly a lord.

"Therefore through following these principles and letting themselves be carried away by conceit they grow arrogant, and they suppose that by haughty countenance and harsh behavior, by ostentatious garments, gold, and jewels, and by almost never letting themselves be seen in public they acquire prestige among men and are almost considered Gods. . . .

8. *Ignorance of the art of governing is pernicious in princes.*

"But if they resolved to know and to do what they ought, they would struggle as hard not to rule as they now struggle to rule, because they would understand how monstrous and pernicious a thing it is that subjects, who are to be governed, should be wiser than the princes, who are to govern. We see that our lack of skill in music, dancing, or riding hurts none of our fellows; nevertheless a person who is not a musician feels shame and does not dare to sing before others; a person who does not know how to dance, will not dance before others; and a person who does not sit a horse well, will not ride. But from not knowing how to govern the people comes so much evil, death, destruction, conflagration, and ruin that it can be called the most deadly plague which is to be found on earth; and yet some princes who are completely ignorant of government are not ashamed to govern, not, shall we say, in the presence of four or of six men, but in the sight of the whole world, since their station is set so high that all eyes gaze upon them and therefore not merely the greatest but even the most insignificant of their shortcomings are observed. . . . But should there come before some of our princes a stern philosopher or anyone at all who desired to reveal to them openly and without art of any sort the terrible face of the true worth and teach them good habits and what sort of life a good prince ought to lead, I am certain that at first sight they would loathe him as they would an asp or indeed mock him as something utterly base.

9. The Courtier should instill love of truth and virtue in his prince's mind.

"I say, then, that since the princes of today are so corrupted by evil habits and by ignorance and false conceit, and since it is so difficult to acquaint them with truth and entice them to virtue, and since men seek to get into their good graces by lies and flattery and similar vicious methods: the Courtier, by means of those noble attributes which Count Ludovico and Messer Federico have given him, easily can and should win for himself the good will of his prince and captivate his mind to the point where the Courtier is given free and safe access to speak to his prince on any subject without being offensive. And if the Courtier is such as he has been described, he will accomplish this with little effort and thus always be able to disclose tactfully to his prince the truth of all matters. In addition to this the Courtier will be able little by little to instill goodness in the prince's mind and teach him continence, fortitude, justice, and temperance, causing him to taste how much sweetness is hidden under that modicum of bitterness which at first sight presents itself to one who struggles against vices. . . ."

11. Can virtue be learned?

Lord Ottaviano fell silent as if he had not wanted to speak further, but Lord Gaspar said:

"I do not believe, Lord Ottaviano, that this goodness of soul, continence, and the other virtues, which you desire the Courtier to teach his lord, are capable of being learned; rather I believe that they are given by nature and by God to those men who possess them. And as evidence that this is so, notice that there is no one in the world so scoundrelly and so misbegotten, no one so dissolute or so unjust, that he will confess he is so upon being asked. On the contrary, each one, however wicked, is pleased to be thought just, sober, and good. This would not happen if these virtues could be learned; for there is no shame in not knowing a thing to which one has not devoted study, but it does indeed appear a reproach not to have something with which we ought to be endowed by nature. Therefore everyone tries to conceal natural defects, of the mind as well as of the body, as we observe in the blind, the lame, the crooked, and others deformed and ugly; for although these defects can be imputed to Nature, still it is distasteful to everyone to recognize them in himself, since one seems to possess that blemish by way of testimonial of that self-same Nature, as if it were a seal and sign of one's malevolence. . . .

12. Virtue can be acquired through habit.

Then Lord Ottaviano said, somewhat laughingly,

"Do you profess, then, Lord Gaspar, that men are so unfortunate and so corrupted in judgment that they have by ingenuity discovered an art for taming the natures of wild beasts such as bears, wolves, and lions and can with that art teach a pretty bird to fly in obedience to man's will and return from the woods and from its natural liberty to leashes and bondage, and that with the same ingenuity they cannot discover or have no desire to discover arts through which they may benefit themselves and, with application and study, improve their mind? . . .

"I think, then, that the moral virtues in us are not wholly from nature, because nothing can become habituated to what is naturally contrary to it, as one sees in a stone, which, though it were thrown upward a full ten thousand times, would never become habituated to go there of itself. Therefore if the virtues were as natural to us as weight is to the stone, we should never become habituated to vice. Nor yet are the vices natural after this fashion, because we should never be able to be virtuous; and it would be monstrous wickedness and stupidity to punish men for those defects which proceed from nature without our fault. And the laws would be guilty of this very error, for they do not impose punishment upon evildoers for the past error, since what has been done cannot be undone, but are concerned with the future, to the end that he who has erred will not err again or will not be the cause that others err through his bad example. And thus the laws take the position that the virtues can be learned, which is perfectly true. For we are born fitted to receive the virtues and the vices likewise, and therefore the propensity toward the one or the other of them is formed in us by habit, in such a way that first we practice the virtues or the vices and afterward we become virtuous or vicious. . . .

13. Ottaviano asserts that men never choose evil as evil.

"Thus, as in the other arts so also in the virtues we must have a teacher who by learning and good advice arouses and awakens in us those moral virtues the seed of which we possess shut away and buried in the soul. . . . For if good and evil were well recognized and understood, everyone would always choose the good and shun the evil. Therefore virtue might almost be called a form of practical wisdom and a knowledge of how to choose the good, and vice a lack of practical wisdom and an ignorance which leads us to judge falsely. For men never choose evil with the idea that it is evil but are deceived by a certain likeness to good.

14. His assertion is challenged but he reaffirms its truth.

Then Lord Gaspar replied:

"There are, however, many people who know clearly that they are doing evil and yet do it; and they do this because the present pleasure that they feel is more important to them than the punishment which they expect they will have to suffer because of it—such men as thieves, murderers, and others of like sort."

Lord Ottaviano said:

"True pleasure is always good and true suffering evil;

however, these men are deceived in mistaking the false pleasure for the true and the true suffering for the false; for which reason, through false pleasures they often fall into true displeasures. That art, then, which teaches how to distinguish this truth from falsity can also be learned; and the virtue by which we choose what is truly good, not what falsely appears to be, can be called true knowledge, a knowledge more beneficial to human life than any other, because it banishes ignorance, from which, as I have said, all evils arise."

15. Bembo objects: "The incontinent know they are choosing evil."

Then Messer Pietro Bembo said:

"I do not know, Lord Ottaviano, how Lord Gaspar can be required to grant you that all evils arise from ignorance and that there are not plenty of people who know quite well that they are sinning when they sin and who are not in the least deceived about the true sorrow. For it is certain that those who are incontinent judge according to reason and judge correctly, and know that the thing to which they are impelled by lust contrary to duty is evil; and yet they resist and set reason against appetite, from which arises the conflict of pleasure and pain against judgment. Ultimately reason, conquered by too powerful appetite, gives up like a ship which defends itself for a while against the tempests at sea, and which in the end, battered by too furious violence of the winds, with anchors and shrouds broken, lets itself be carried at the caprice of fortune, without use of rudder or any direction from the compass to save her.

"The incontinent therefore commit their mistakes with a kind of wavering compunction and, as it were, in spite of themselves. They would not do this if they failed to see that what they are doing is evil and followed absolutely headlong after appetite without any opposition from reason; in that case they would be not incontinent but intemperate. . . ."

16. Ottaviano replies that the incontinent do not fully know evil as evil.

Signor Ottaviano replied:

"Indeed, Messer Pietro, you put up a good argument; nevertheless, in my opinion it is more plausible than sound. For though the incontinent sin with that wavering, though reason contends with appetite in their minds, and though they recognize what is evil as evil, still they do not possess complete comprehension and do not know evil as fully as is necessary; therefore there exists in these people a weak opinion rather than certain knowledge concerning evil, which is why they allow reason to be overpowered by passion. But if they had true knowledge of evil, there is no doubt but that they would not err. For it is always ignorance through which the appetite conquers reason, and true knowledge can never be overcome by passion, which has its source in the body and not in the mind and which, if it is well ruled and controlled by reason, becomes virtue, whereas otherwise it becomes vice. But reason has such great power that it always makes itself obeyed by sense and penetrates by wonderful means and paths, provided ignorance is not in possession of the territory that reason ought to possess. In this fashion, although the spirits and the nerves and the bones do not in themselves possess reason, still when that movement of the mind arises in us, almost as if thought set spur to the spirits and shook the reins, all the members make ready, the feet to run and the hands to grasp or to do whatever the mind proposes; and this fact is also clearly observed in many who, without knowing it, on occasion eat some loathsome and nasty food which seems very dainty to their palate; then upon learning what it was, not only do they feel pain and distress in their minds, but the body agrees so well with the judgment of the mind that they perforce vomit up that food. . . ."

17-18. Ottaviano discourses on temperance.

At this point there is a digression concerning temperance, which Lord Ottaviano calls the source of many other virtues. If the Courtier follows Ottaviano's prescriptions he will see all the virtues spring up in the mind of the prince, especially the greatest virtue, the science of good government, which could bring back to the earth the Age of Gold.

19. Is the monarchical to be preferred to the republican form of government?

Lord Ottaviano having paused a moment at this point as if to rest, Lord Gaspar said:

"Lord Ottaviano, which do you think the happier form of government and the one better able to restore to the world that Golden Age you mentioned: the rule of so good a prince or the government of a good republic?"

Lord Ottaviano answered:

"I should always prefer the rule of a good prince, because that is the dominion more in accordance with nature and, if it is permissible to compare small things with infinite ones, more like that of God, who singly and solely rules the universe. But leaving this argument aside, observe that in what is created by human art, such as armies, great navies, buildings, and similar things, everything is referred back to a single person who governs in his own fashion. Likewise in our body the members labor and function at the command of the heart. Besides this, it seems fitting that the people be governed thus by a prince as are also many animals, to which nature teaches this obedience as a very salutary thing. See how the deer, the cranes, and many other birds when they make a journey always place at their head a prince, whom they follow and obey; and how the bees serve their monarch almost with a power of reasoning and with as much reverence as the most obedient people in the world; and this then is a very strong argument that the rule of princes is more in accordance with nature than that of republics."

20. Bembo prefers the republican form.

Then Messer Pietro Bembo said:

"And it seems to me that since liberty has been given to us by God as supreme gift, it is not reasonable that it be taken from us or that one man enjoy more of it than another, as happens under the rule of princes, who for the most part hold the subjects in strictest dependence. But in well ordered republics one still enjoys this liberty. Besides, it happens both in decisions and in deliberations that the opinion of a single person is more often mistaken than the opinion of many people, because turmoil, occasioned by anger or by scorn or by covetousness, invades the mind of a single person more easily than that of the multitude, much as a great body of water is less subject to becoming tainted than a small one.

"I say also that the example of the animals does not seem to me to apply; because both deer and cranes and the others do not always prefer to follow and obey the same individual; rather they change and shift this dominion, giving it now to one and now to another; and in such fashion it comes to approximate closer the form of republic than of kingdom. And this can be called true and equal liberty when those who at one time command at another time obey. Likewise the example of the bees does not seem parallel to me, because that monarch of theirs is not of their own species, and therefore one who would wish to give to men a truly worthy lord will have to find him among another species and of a nature more excellent than human, if men are reasonably expected to obey him; just as the herds obey not an animal of their own kind but a shepherd, who is a man and of a species more worthy than theirs. For these reasons, Lord Ottaviano, I regard the government of the republic as more desirable than that of the king."

*21. Ottaviano gives further argument
in favor of monarchy.*

Then Lord Ottaviano said:

"Against your view, Messer Pietro, I only wish to adduce one reason, which is that there are only three methods of governing the people well. One is monarchy; the second is the government by the good, whom the ancients used to call *optimates;* the other is administration by the people. And the violations and contrary vices, so to speak, into which each of these forms of government passes by being undermined and corrupted, exist when monarchy becomes tyranny, when the government of the good is transformed into that of a few powerful men who are not good, and when administration by the people is seized by the lower classes who, in destroying class distinctions, submit the government of the state as a whole to the will of the multitude. Of these three evil forms of government it is certain that tyranny is the worst of all, as can be proved by many reasons. It remains then that of the three good forms, monarchy is the best, because it is the opposite of the worst form: for, as you know, the effects of contrary causes are themselves also the contraries of each other.

"Now concerning what you have said about liberty, I answer that one should not define true liberty as 'living as one pleases' but as 'living according to good laws;' nor is obeying less natural and useful and necessary than commanding; and certain things are created, and thus singled out and ordained by nature, to command, as certain others to obey. It is true that there are two ways of exercising lordship: the one imperious and violent, such as that of masters over slaves; and with this kind the soul exercises authority over the body. The other is more gentle and pacific, such as that of good princes over citizens by means of laws, and with this kind the reason exercises authority over appetite. And both of these ways are useful, because the body is created by nature fitted to obey the soul and likewise appetite to obey reason. There are still many men whose activities center wholly upon bodily functions, and men such as these are as different from virtuous men as the soul is from the body; being rational animals they have a share of reason, but only to the extent that they recognize it, though they do not possess it or profit by it. These therefore are naturally underlings, and it is better and more profitable for them to obey than to command."

22. How princes should exercise authority.

Then Lord Gaspar said:

"In what way then is authority to be exercised over those who are circumspect and virtuous and who are not underlings by nature?"

Lord Ottaviano answered:

"By pacific authority, royal and civil. And it is good policy to entrust such men from time to time with the administration of those offices for which they are fitted, so that they can also exercise authority and govern men less wise than they—in such manner, however, that the chief rule depends wholly on the supreme prince. And since you have said that it is an easier thing for the mind of a single man to become corrupt than that of many, I reply that it is a still easier thing to find one good and wise man than many; and we should hold that a king can be good and wise who is of noble stock, inclined to virtue by natural instinct and by the famous memory of his ancestors, and trained in good habits. And though he is not of a species greater than human, as you have described the ruler of the bees, yet, because he has been strengthened by the discipline and art of the Courtier, a man formed so wise and good by these lords, he will be in the highest degree just, continent, temperate, manly, and wise, filled with liberality, majesty, religion, and mercy; in short he will be surpassingly glorious and exceedingly beloved by men and by God, through whose grace he will obtain that heroic virtue which will make him transcend the limits of human nature and deserve to be called demigod rather than mortal man. . . ."

25-26. The prince ought to follow the contemplative more than the active life.

Then Lord Gaspar said:

"And which of the two lives [the active life and the contemplative life] seems to you, Lord Ottaviano, to be more fitting for the prince? . . .

Lord Ottaviano replied:

". . . I say that the prince ought to cultivate both lives, but more, however, the contemplative, because for princes this life has two sides, one of which consists in understanding and judging well, the other in comanding, justly and by methods that are fitting, things that are within reason and that fall within his authority, and in imposing his commands at proper places and times upon those who may reasonably be bound to obey. And Duke Federico was speaking of this matter when he said that the man who knows how to command is always obeyed. For to command is always the principal duty of princes, who furthermore ought frequently to observe with their own eyes and be present at the execution of their commands, and according to the times and requirements now and again also take action themselves. All this, however, partakes of activity. But the end of the active life should be the contemplative, as peace is the end of war and repose of toil.

27. Subjects should be habituated to a life of peace.

"Therefore it is also the duty of the good prince to train his people in such ways and through such laws and decrees, that they may live in ease and in peace, without danger and with dignity, and enjoy commendably this end of their activities, which ought to be tranquility. For there have been many republics and monarchs which consistently have been extremely prosperous and great in war, and just as soon as they have attained peace they have gone to ruin and lost the greatness and splendor like unused iron. And this has happened solely from lack of good training in living in peace and from ignorance of how to enjoy the blessing of leisure. Also it is not lawful always to be at war without seeking to arrive at the end, peace, although there are some princes who think that their purpose ought chiefly to be that of ruling over their neighbors and who therefore nurture in their people a warlike and ferocious appetite for plunder, slaughter, and things of this sort, give them rewards to arouse it, and call it virtue. In accordance with this policy it used to be the custom among the Scythians that a man who had not killed an enemy could not drink from the cup that was carried around the company at solemn feasts. In other places the custom was to erect around the tomb as many obelisks as there were enemies slain by the man buried there; and all these practices and others like them were observed in order to make the men warlike, solely with the aim of ruling over others. This aim was almost impossible of attainment, since it was an undertaking without limits, lasting to the point where the entire world would have been subjugated, and very deficient in reason, according to the law of nature, which does not consent that we should take pleasure in seeing others suffer what we should be displeased to suffer ourselves.

"Therefore princes should make the people warlike not to indulge lust for dominion but to win the power to defend themselves and their people from anyone who wishes to reduce them to bondage or do them wrong in any respect whatsoever; or to expel tyrants and govern well those people who have been badly treated; or to reduce to dependence those who are of such nature that they deserve to be made slaves, with the purpose of governing them well and bringing leisure, response, and peace to them. . . ."

28. What virtues are requisite in war and in peace?

Then Lord Gaspar said:

"I should like to know which virtues are useful and requisite in war and which worthy in peace."

Lord Ottaviano replied:

"All are good and helpful, because they are directed toward a good end; however, especially valuable in war is that true fortitude which renders the mind so free from passions that it not only does not fear dangers but even ignores them; likewise, constancy and that enduring patience with mind fixed and unperturbed by all the blows of fortune. It behooves us, also, in war and at all times, to possess all the virtues that aim at probity, such as justice, continence, and temperance, but much more in times of peace and in ease, because often men who are placed in prosperity and in ease and who think fortune smiles on them become unjust and intemperate and allow themselves to be corrupted by pleasure. Therefore men placed in such circumstances have the greatest need of those virtues, because ease too readily instills evil habits in human minds. . . ."

29. The prince is to be taught virtue first by habit, then by precept.

Then Lord Gaspar said:

"Lord Ottaviano, since you have greatly extolled good education and appear almost to believe that this is the chief means for making a man virtuous and honorable, I would like to know if that training which the Courtier is to give his prince should be begun with custom and as it were with daily habits, which confirm him in proper behavior without his perceiving it; or if the Courtier ought rather to begin by demonstrating to the prince through reason the nature of good and evil and, before the prince has set out on his journey, to make known to him which is the good path and the one to follow and which the bad and the one to avoid; in short, whether virtue should first be instilled and established in his mind by reason and understanding or by habituation."

Said Lord Ottaviano:

"You are setting me out on too long a discourse. However, so that you will not think I fail you because I do not care to answer your question, I say that as the mind and the body are two entities in use, so also the soul is divided in two parts, one of which contains in itself the reason, the other the appetite. Now just as in generation the body precedes the soul, so the irrational part of the soul precedes the rational, something which is clearly perceived in children, in whom anger and delight are evidenced almost as soon as the children are born, whereas reason appears after a space of time. Therefore we ought to make the body our care earlier than the soul, and then the appetite earlier than the reason—the care of the body, however, for the sake of the soul, and the care of the appetite for the sake of reason. For as the intellectual virtue is perfected by teaching, so the moral virtue is perfected by habit.

"Hence we ought first to teach through habit, which is able to govern the appetites when they are as yet not susceptible to reason and to direct them to the good by right custom, and afterwards we ought to confirm them through intelligence which, although it shows its light later, nevertheless offers to one whose mind is well trained through habits (on which, in my opinion, the whole matter depends) a means of possessing the virtues in greater perfection. . . .

31. The lower orders should be given a share in the government.

"Many other things, Madame, I would teach . . . the prince if I knew them, and, among the others, that from among his subjects he choose a number of the noblest and wisest gentlemen with whom to deliberate every matter, and grant them a license and full freedom that will enable them to tell him their opinion frankly on all subjects. And he should assume with them a manner which will make them all perceive that he desires to know the truth in every matter and that he holds all falsehood in detestation; and in addition to this council of the nobles I should recommend that other men of lesser rank be chosen from the people, of whom a popular council would be formed which would confer with the council of nobles concerning the needs of the city, in both the public and private spheres. And in this fashion, with the prince as head and the nobles and common people as the members, there would be constituted a single body knit together, the government of which would derive chiefly from the prince yet would also be shared in by the others. And thus this state would have the structure of three good governments, namely the Monarchy, Optimates, and People.

32. The chief responsibility of a prince is justice.

"Next, I would show him that among the reponsibilities which belong to the prince the most important is that of justice; for the conservation of which there would be chosen as magistrates men wise and well tested whose wisdom is true wisdom accompanied by probity, because otherwise it is not wisdom but cunning. And when probity is missing, the art and subtlety of lawyers spells nothing but ruin and doom for the laws and the judicial decisions, and the blame for every one of the failings of these men is to be imputed to him who put them in office.

"I should declare how from justice there also proceeds that piety toward God which is obligatory upon all and especially upon princes, who ought to love Him above every other thing and direct all their actions to him as the true end and, as Xenophanes said, to honor him and love him always, but much more when they are in prosperity, in order afterwards more justifiably to make bold to ask assistance of Him in some adversity; for it is impossible to govern either oneself or others without aid of God. . . .

33. What measure of liberty and wealth should be permitted to subjects?

"Next I would declare how he ought to love his native land and his people, not maintaining them in too strict dependence, in order not to make himself odious to them, the condition from which seditions, conspiracies, and a thousand other evils take their origin; nor in too great liberty, either, in order not to be held in contempt, the condition from which proceed licentious and dissolute living among the people, plunder, theft, and murder, in the complete absence of fear of the laws, and often the ruin and total subversion of the city and dominions.

"Next, I would declare how he ought to cherish those near him in every degree, treating all in certain matters with even equality, as in justice and liberty, and in some other matters with a just inequality, as in liberality, in recompensing, and in distributing honors and distinctions according to the inequality of merits, which never ought to exceed but always be exceeded by the recompense; and that in this way he would be not merely loved but almost adored by his subjects, nor would he be obliged to entrust himself to foreigners for the preservation of his life; for in their proper interest his own people would guard his life with their own. . . . And thus the minds of the citizens will be so tempered that the good ones will not try to have more than they need and the evil will not be able to. For in many instances excessive riches are the cause of great ruin, as in unhappy Italy, which has been and at present is a prey exposed to foreign nations, as much because of bad government as because of the great riches with which she teems.

"Therefore it were well that the greater part of the citizens were neither very rich nor very poor, because those who are too rich often become arrogant and rash, while the poor become base and fraudulent; but those of moderate means lay no snares for others and live secure from being ensnared. And since those of moderate means are greater in number, they are also more powerful; and therefore neither the poor nor the rich can conspire against the prince, or against others, or create seditions. Hence in order to escape this evil it is very salutary to preserve everywhere the middle state.

34. Civil discontent springs from subjects' hatred or contempt of the prince.

"I would declare then that a prince ought to employ these and many other timely remedies, so that desire of innovations and of change of rule should not arise in the mind of the subjects. These are things which subjects effect sometimes for the sake of gain or honor that they hope for, at other times because of loss or disgrace that they fear; and these agitations in their minds are generated at times by hate and wrath which make men desperate, owing to the injuries and abuses which are visited on them through the avarice, pride, and cruelty or lustfulness of their overlords; at times by the contempt which is aroused in them by the negligence, baseness, and ineptitude of princes. And these two mistakes ought to be avoided by winning affection and approval from the people, something which can be accomplished by rewarding and honoring the good and by improving conditions wisely and sometimes with severity so that the wicked and seditious do not become powerful. . . ."

36. It is objected that the Courtier's highest end is to encourage princes in magnificence.

For a long time the Duchess and Lady Emilia and all the others had remained closely attentive to the discourse of Lord Ottaviano, but when he made a brief pause at this point, as if he had terminated his discourse, Messer Cesare Gonzaga said:

"In truth, Lord Ottaviano, it cannot be asserted that your teachings are not good and useful. Nevertheless, I should think that if you formed your prince by these teachings, you would more nearly deserve the name of good schoolmaster than of good Courtier, and he more nearly the name of good governor than of great prince. I do not indeed assert that it ought not to be the responsibility of rulers that the people are well ruled by justice and good customs; nevertheless, I think that it is enough for rulers to choose good ministers to carry out matters of this sort and that the true duty of rulers is something much weightier. Therefore, if I believed myself to be that excellent Courtier which these lords have delineated and to possess the favor of my prince, it is certain that I would not seduce him to any vicious practice; rather, in order to attain that good end which you describe and which I agree should be the fruit of the toils and activities of the Courtier, I should seek to stamp on the prince's mind a certain grandeur together with that regal magnificence, readiness of mind, and invincible valor in arms which should make him loved and revered by everyone of whatsoever class, so that he should be famous and illustrious in the world chiefly through this grandeur. I should say also that he should couple with grandeur a familiar gentleness, together with a winning and friendly humanity and polished manner of caressing both subjects and foreigners with discretion and in greater or lesser measure according to their merits, always preserving, however, the majesty which befits his rank and which should never permit his prestige to be impaired in any respect through too great humility, though it should never arouse hatred of him through too harsh a severity. He ought to be most generous and munificent and give to each without reserve, because God, as they say, is the treasurer of generous princes. He should present magnificent banquets, revels, games, and public shows and have a great number of excellent horses for use in war and for delight in peace, as well as falcons, dogs, and all other things that enter into the diversions of great lords and of the people—such as in our times we have seen to be the practice of Lord Francesco Gonzaga, Marquis of Mantua, who in these matters seems rather king of Italy than ruler of a city.

"I would try also to induce the prince to erect great buildings both to bring him honor during his lifetime and to perpetuate his memory for posterity, as Duke Federico did in this noble palace and Pope Julius is at present doing in the church of Saint Peter and that street which runs from the Palace to the Belvedere summerhouse, and in many other buildings; as also the ancient Romans used to do, of whom we see so many remains at Rome, at Naples, at Pozzuoli, at Baiae, at Civita Vecchia, at Porto, and likewise outside Italy and in a great many other places that bear magnificent witness to the powers of those transcendent minds. . . .

49. Can the Courtier be a lover?

Lord Gaspar then said:

"In discoursing on the attributes of the Courtier last evening these lords desired that he should be in love. And since in summing up what has been said so far one would draw a conclusion that the Courtier, who has to lead his prince to virtue by his own worth and credit, must almost of necessity be old—for only in very rare instances does knowledge arrive before age does, and especially in those matters which are learned through experience—I do not see how being in love can become him, if he is advanced in years, considering that . . . love does not prosper in the old, and those things which in youth are attractive—courtesies and refinements in dress so dear to the ladies—are in these men insanities and ridiculous improprieties and produce odium from the ladies and mockery from the others for anyone who employs them. Therefore if this Aristotle of yours, as an elderly Courtier, were in love and did those things which young men in love do, as some we have seen in our times, I fear that he would forget to instruct his prince, and perhaps the children would mock him behind his back and the women would find no other pleasure in him except to make him an object of jests."

Thereupon Lord Ottaviano said:

"Since all the other attributes assigned to the Courtier are appropriate for him even though he be old, I do not really think that we ought to deprive him of the happiness of loving."

"On the contrary," said Lord Gaspar, "to deprive him of this love is one perfection the more and a way to make him live happily, exempt from distress and misfortune."

50. The kind of love appropriate to the Courtier.

Said Messer Pietro Bembo:

"Do you not recall, Lord Gaspar, that Lord Ottaviano, even though little skilled in love, nevertheless in his game the other evening showed his knowledge that there are some lovers who count as sweet the scorn and wrath and battle and torment that they suffer at the hands of their ladies, for which reason he asked to be taught the cause of this sweetness? If therefore our Courtier, though elderly, were kindled by those loves which are sweet without admixture of bitterness, he should not think it a catastrophe or any kind of sorrow, and being wise as we are supposing him to be, he would not be misled into thinking that everything which might be suitable for young men would be suitable for him, but in loving he should perhaps love in a fashion that would bring him no reproach and even much approval, along with supreme happiness unattended by the slightest grief, something which rarely or almost never falls to the lot of the young; and thus he would not slacken in instructing his prince nor would he do anything which deserved the mockery of children."

Then the Duchess said:

"I am glad, Messer Pietro, that you have had little employment in our discourses this evening, because we shall with the greater assurance now impose upon you the task of speaking and of teaching the Courtier this love which is so happy that it carries with it neither reproach nor distress. For it will perhaps turn out to be one of the most important and useful attributes that have as yet been assigned to him. Therefore declare on your faith all that you know about it."

Messer Pietro laughed and said:

"I should not like it, Madame, if my saying that it is permissible for old men to love were the cause of my being taken for an old man by these ladies; therefore assign this task to another instead."

The Duchess replied:

"You ought not refuse to be held old in wisdom though you be young in years; so speak and try no more to have yourself excused."

Messer Pietro said:

"Truly, Madame, since I am obliged to talk about this subject, I ought to go ask counsel of the Hermit of my Lavinello."

The Lady Emilia said, as if annoyed:

"Messer Pietro, there is no one in the company who is more disobedient than you. It will be well if the Duchess assigns you some punishment."

Messer Pietro said, laughing:

"Do not get angry with me, Madame, for the love of God; for I will say what you wish."

"Say it, then," answered Lady Emilia.

51. What is love?

Thereupon Messer Pietro, after first falling silent for awhile, then settling himself a little as if to speak of an important matter, said as follows:

"Lords, in order to show that the old can love not only without reproach but also with greater happiness sometimes than the young, I shall be obliged to deliver a short discourse designed to make clear what love is and what the happiness is which lovers can possess. Therefore I beg you to listen to me with attention, because I hope to make you see that there is no man to whom being in love is unbecoming, even though he were fifteen or twenty years older than Lord Morello."

And when they had laughed over this a little while, Messer Pietro continued:

"I declare then that, as it is defined by the wise ancients, love is nothing else than a certain desire to enjoy beauty, and because desire has appetite only for things known, knowledge must always precede desire, which by its nature seeks the good but in itself is blind and does not know the good. Therefore nature has so ordained that to every cognitive power there is joined an appetitive power, and since in our soul there are three ways of knowing, namely through sense, through reason, and through understanding, we find that from sense arises appetite, which we have in common with the unreasoning beasts, from reason springs choice, which is peculiar to man, and from understanding, through which man can have communication with the angels, springs will. Thus, then, as sense knows only things capable of being perceived by the senses, appetite desires only these same things; and just as understanding is turned only to the contemplation of things that are intelligible, our will is fed only on spiritual good. Man, rational by nature, placed as mean between these two extremes, can through his choice, by descending to sense or rising to understanding, side with the desires of the one or the other element. In these ways then one can desire beauty, the generic term for which is applicable to all things, whether natural or artificial, which are formed with good proportion and proper constitution in so far as their nature allows.

52. Sensual love does not bring satisfaction.

"But in speaking of the beauty that we have had in mind, which is solely that which appears in human bodies and especially in human countenances and stirs this burning desire that we call love, we will say that it is efflux of the divine goodness, which, though spread over all created

things like the light of the sun, still, when it finds a countenance that is well proportioned and formed with a certain
joyous harmony of various colors set off by lights and
shadows and by a well-ordered spacing and limit of con-
tours, infuses itself there and appears in full beauty; and
with a wonderful grace and splendor it embellishes and illu-
minates that object on which it shines in the manner of a
sunbeam, which strikes upon a beautiful vessel of burnished
gold set with precious gems, in such fashion that it pleasur-
ably attracts men's eyes to itself and penetrating through
them, impresses itself upon the soul and stirs and delights her
throughout with a new charm and by setting the soul afire
causes itself to be desired by her.

"If the soul, upon being possessed by the desire to
enjoy this beauty as something good, allows itself to be
guided by the judgment of sense, it falls into the gravest of
errors and judges that the body in which the beauty is perceived is the principal cause of that beauty, for which reason
it thinks that in order to enjoy that beauty it must unite as
intimately as possible with the body. This is untrue; and so
whoever thinks that he can enjoy beauty by possessing the
body is deceived and is moved not by true knowledge
through the choice of reason but by false opinion through
the appetite of sense. For this reason the pleasure which
follows such possession is itself necessarily false and imperfect. And therefore all those lovers who satisfy their
unchaste wishes with the women they love encounter one
of two evils. For as soon as they reach the desired end they
not only feel satiety and disgust but come to hate the loved
object, as if appetite repented its error and recognized the
deception visited upon it by the false judgment of sense
through which it believed that what was evil was good; or
on the other hand they continue in the same desire and
hunger, like those who have not truly reached the end they
were seeking; and although by virtue of the blind opinion by
which they are intoxicated they think that they find pleasure
at that moment, like sick people who sometimes dream of

drinking at some clear spring, nevertheless they are not satisfied or appeased.

"And since from the possession of a desired good, peace and contentment always arise in the mind of the possessor, it follows that if physical enjoyment were the true and good end of their desire, they too would remain in peace and contentment by possessing it, something they do not do. On the contrary, misled by that semblance, they quickly return to unrestrained desire; and, with the same vexation which they felt before, they find themselves again beset with the wild and burning thirst for that which in vain they hope to possess in its fullness. Such lovers as these, then, love most unhappily, for either they do not attain what they desire and suffer great unhappiness; or if they attain it, they find they have attained what is evil for them, and they extinguish their sufferings in other sufferings yet greater. For in the beginning and still at the midpoint of this love nothing else is experienced but anguish, torment, sorrow, privation, and toil, to the point that to be wan, suffering, ceaselessly in tears and sighs, to be melancholy, to be always mute or lamenting, to want to die, in short to be as miserable as possible, are the traits said to characterize lovers.

53. *The cause of sensuality.*

"The cause, then, of this disaster to human minds is chiefly sense, which in youth is all-powerful because the strength of the flesh and of the blood in that season gives sense as much force as it takes away from reason and so easily persuades the soul to follow appetite; for the soul, finding herself shut up in the earthly prison and deprived of contemplation of things spiritual, cannot by herself clearly grasp the truth. Hence, in order to understand these things, she must go begging the first notion from the senses and therefore believe them and defer to them and let herself be guided by them, particularly when they are so powerful that they almost compel her. And because they are deceitful they fill her with errors and false opinions.

"For this reason it almost always happens that young people are wrapped up in this sensual love which is wholly rebellious to reason, and therefore they render themselves unworthy of enjoying the favors and the blessing which love bestows on its true subjects; nor do they experience in love pleasures beyond the same ones that irrational animals experience, while experiencing much deeper anguish.

"Assuming this to be the case, then, as it most truly is, I say that the contrary happens to those who are of more mature age; for if, at the time when the soul is not greatly weighed down by the burden of the flesh and the natural heat begins to grow cooler, men such as these are fired by beauty and turn toward it a desire guided by rational choice, they are not deceived and they possess beauty in its fullness. And for that reason good always comes to them from the enjoyment of it, because beauty is a good and consequently the true love of it is entirely good and holy and always produces good effects in the mind of those who with the reins of reason rectify the obliquity of sense, something that the old can do much more easily than the young.

54. Sensuality can be condoned only in young men.

"It is therefore not unreasonable to say also that the old can love without reproach and more happily than the young, understanding this appellation 'old' not to mean decrepit, however, nor to refer to the time when the bodily organs already are so enfeebled that the soul cannot exercise her powers through them; but to the time when knowledge exists in us in its true strength. I will not pass over in silence a further point, namely that I think that although sensual love is bad at every age, still it deserves to be excused in the young, and perhaps in a certain fashion is permissible; for if indeed it brings them grief, peril, toil, and those sorrows which it has been said to, there are still, however, many men who, in order to win the favor of the women they love, do virtuous things which, although not directed toward a good end, nevertheless are good in themselves; and in this way they extract a little sweetness from that great quantity of bitterness, and through the misfortunes that they undergo they recognize their error in the end. Therefore, just as I believe that those young men who check their appetites and love according to reason are sublime, so also I excuse those who let themselves be conquered by sensual love to which they are so strongly inclined by human weakness—provided that in sensuality they display gentility, courtesy, valor, and the other noble attributes which these lords have mentioned and that, when they are no longer of youthful age, they wholly abandon it, departing from this sensual desire as from the lowest step on the stair by which one can climb to the true love. But if after they are old they yet maintain in the cold heart the fire of appetite and therefore subject vigorous reason to weak sense, one cannot say how much they are to be reproached; for like madmen they deserve to be numbered among the irrational animals in perpetual infamy, because the thoughts and ways of sensual love are extremely unbecoming to mature years."

55. Are beautiful women always good women?

At this point Bembo paused briefly, as if to rest; and as everyone remained silent, Messer Morello da Ortona said:

"And if an old man were found more ardent and lively and better looking than many young men, why do you wish to deny him the right to love with that love with which young men love?"

The Duchess laughed and said:

"If the love of the young is so unfortunate, why do you, Lord Morello, wish the old men also to love with that unhappiness? But were you old, as those gentlemen say, you would not be procuring evil for the old in this fashion."

Lord Morello replied:

"It seems to me that the one who is procuring evil for the old is Messer Pietro Bembo, who wishes to have them love in a certain way which I for one do not understand;

and I think that to enjoy this beauty which he praises so highly, without enjoying the body, is a dream."

"Do you believe, Lord Morello," said then Count Ludovico, "that beauty is always as good as Messer Pietro Bembo declares?"

"I do not in the least," answered Lord Morello; "on the contrary, I recall having seen many beautiful women who were extremely wicked, cruel, and spiteful; and it seems that it nearly always happens thus, because beauty makes them proud, and pride makes them cruel."

Count Ludovico said, laughing:

"Perhaps they seem cruel to you because they do not gratify you with what you would like; but let yourself be instructed by Messer Pietro Bembo concerning the fashion in which old men ought to desire women and what they ought to seek and with what they ought to be satisfied, and if you do not go beyond these bounds you will see that beautiful women are not proud or cruel and that they will gratify you with what you desire."

At this Lord Morello appeared a trifle nettled and said:

"I do not care to know what does not concern me; but do you take instruction yourself in how young men who are less ardent and less vigorous than told men should desire beauty."

56. Bembo affirms that beauty is always good.

At this point Messer Federico, in order to pacify Lord Morello and turn the discussion, did not allow Count Ludovico to answer but said, interrupting him:

"Perhaps Lord Morello is not entirely wrong in saying that beauty is not always good, because oftentimes the beauties of women are the reason that countless ills, enmities, wars, deaths, and devastations occur in the world, of which the ruin of Troy provides good witness, and beautiful women are most often either proud and cruel or, as pointed out, unchaste—though this would not seem a failing to Lord Morello. There are also many men who are scoundrels but have the gift of good looks, and it would seem that nature has made them so in order that they may be the better able to deceive and that the charming exterior should act like the bait that hides the hook beneath."

Then Messer Pietro Bembo said:

"Never believe that beauty is not always good."

Here Count Ludovico, also in order to get back to the original proposition, broke in and said:

"Since Lord Morello is not interested in knowing what is of such concern to him, teach it to me and show me how old men acquire this happiness in love, for I do not care if I make people think I am old, provided I profit by it."

57. Why the beautiful are also good.

Messer Pietro Bembo laughed and said:

"I want first of all to free the minds of these lords from their mistake; then I will satisfy you also."

Beginning again in this way, he said:

"Lords, I am desirous that no one of us should incur the wrath of God by speaking evil of beauty, which is a sacred thing. Therefore, in order that Lord Morello and Messer Federico may be warned and not, like Stesichorus, lose their sight—the punishment most appropriate for one who disparages beauty—I assert that beauty springs from God and is like a circle of which goodness is the center; and therefore, just as there can be no circle without a center there can be no beauty without goodness. For this reason it is a rare thing for an evil soul to dwell in a beautiful body, and therefore external beauty is a certain sign of inner goodness; and that grace is imprinted upon bodies more or less as an index of the soul, by which the soul is known from external signs, as with trees, in which the beauty of the blossoms betokens the goodness of the fruit. And the same thing occurs with bodies, for we find the Physiognomists frequently read the characters and sometimes the thoughts of men in the countenance; and what is more, in the animals also we discern from the face the character of the mind, which expresses itself in the body as fully as it can. Think how clearly we recognize wrath, ferocity, and pride in the countenance of the lion, the horse and the eagle; in lambs and doves a pure and simple innocence; in wolves and foxes crafty malice, and so on in almost all the other animals.

58. Beauty is consistent with utility.

"The ugly therefore are also for the most part wicked and the beautiful good; and it can be said that beauty is the pleasing, happy, welcome, and winning face of good; and ugliness the dark, disturbing, displeasing, and sorrowful face of evil; and if you give heed to things you will always find that those things which are good and useful possess also the grace of beauty. Consider the constitution of this great mechanism of the world, which was fashioned by God for the welfare and preservation of all created things. The ensphering heaven, embellished by so many divine lights, and at the center the earth compassed about by the elements and sustained by its own weight; the sun, which in his circuit lights the whole and in winter moves towards the lowest sign, then little by little ascends to the other region; the moon, which receives her light from the sun, according to whether the sun approaches or moves away from her; and the five other stars which in various fashions follow the same course. These exercise such influence on each other through interconnection of an order founded in necessity, that if they were altered in the least particular they could not hold together and would reduce the world to ruins. They possess also such a great beauty and grace that human wits cannot imagine a thing more beautiful. Think now of the figure of man which can be termed a world in little, in which each part of the body is seen to be set in place according to necessity, through art and not through chance, and the entire form altogether is seen to be extremely beautiful—so much so that only with difficulty could we decide whether all the members, such as the eyes, the arms, the breast, and likewise the other parts, contribute to the human countenance and the rest of the body more usefulness or more grace. Observe the feathers of birds, the leaves and branches of trees, which are bestowed on them by nature to preserve their being and yet have also very great loveliness. Leave nature and come to art. What thing is so indispensable in ships as the prow, the sides, the sailyards, the mast, the sails, the rudder, the oars, the anchor, and the shrouds? All these things, however, possess so much beauty that it seems to one who looks at them that they are as much devised for the sake of pleasing as for usefulness. Columns and architraves support the lofty galleries and palaces; in being useful to the buildings they are none the less pleasing to the eyes of one who looks at them. When men first began to build, they placed that ridge down the middle, not because the buildings would have greater grace, but so that the water might run off more conveniently from either side; nevertheless, beauty was quickly added to utility, so that even if a temple were constructed under a sky from which neither hail nor rain fell, it would seem incapable of having any distinction or beauty without the ridge.

59. The good and the beautiful are in some sense the same.

"Much praise therefore is given to the world, as well as to other things, by saying that it is beautiful. It is praised by our saying *beautiful heaven, beautiful earth, beautiful sea, beautiful rivers, beautiful countrysides, beautiful woodlands, trees, gardens, beautiful cities, beautiful temples, houses, armies*. In short, this gracious and holy beauty confers supreme embellishment on everything; and it can be said that the good and the beautiful are in some fashion the same thing, and especially in human bodies, for I consider the immediate cause of their beauty to be the beauty of the soul, which, since it participates in that true divine beauty, illumines and renders beautiful whatever it touches, especially if that body in which it resides is not of such base matter that the soul cannot imprint upon it her character. Therefore beauty is the true trophy of the soul when she through divine power reigns over material nature and with her light conquers the shadows of the body.

"Thus we are not to say that beauty makes women proud or cruel, although it seems so to Messer Morello; nor should we attribute to beautiful women those enmities, deaths, and devastations which are caused by the immoderate appetites of men. I will not in the least deny that it is possible to find in the world some women who are beautiful but who are also unchaste, but it is not at all because beauty disposes them to lewdness; on the contrary, it leads them away and draws them to the path of virtuous manners through the relationship that beauty has with goodness. But sometimes poor upbringing, the continuous urgings of lovers, gifts, poverty, hope, deception, fear and a thousand other causes overcome the steadfastness even of beautiful and good women; and for these or similar causes beautiful men may also become depraved."

60. Sensual appeal should not be mistaken for beauty.

Then Messer Cesar said:

"If what Lord Gaspar alleged yesterday is true, there is no doubt that the beautiful are chaster than the ugly."

"And what thing did I allege?" said Lord Gaspar.

Messer Cesare replied:

"If I remember correctly, you said that women who are courted always refuse to gratify the man who courts them; and those who are not courted court others. It is certain that the beautiful ones are always more courted and solicited for their love than the ugly ones. Therefore the beautiful ones always deny and consequently are chaster than the ugly, who, not being courted themselves, court others."

Bembo laughed and said:

"This argument cannot be answered." Then he added: "It also happens frequently that our vision, quite like our other senses, is deceived and takes for beautiful a face which in reality is not beautiful; and because we sometimes see in the eyes and in the whole expression of some women a certain sensuality portrayed with wanton enticements, many men, who are pleased by such behavior because it promises ease in the attainment of what they desire, call this beauty; but in reality it is a disguised lewdness, unworthy of so honored and holy a name."

Messer Pietro Bembo fell silent; those lords, however, urged him to speak further of this love and of the way to enjoy beauty rightly; and he finally said:

"It seems to me that I have quite clearly shown that the old can love more happily than the young, which was what I set out to do; therefore it is not proper for me to go on."

Count Ludovico replied:

"You have more thoroughly set forth the misery of young men than the happiness of the old, to whom you have not yet taught what path they have to follow in this love of theirs; you have only said that they are to let themselves be guided by reason; and by many it is thought impossible that love should be consistent with reason."

61. Bembo undertakes to describe the love that transcends sensuality.

Bembo still endeavored to bring the discourse to an end, but the Duchess begged him to speak and he began again thus:

"Human nature would be most unfortunate if our soul, in which such intense desire can easily be kindled, were compelled to feed it only with what she has in common with the beasts and could not turn it to that nobler part which is peculiarly hers. Therefore, since it is indeed your pleasure to have it so, I do not wish to shun discourse on this noble subject. And because I know that I am not worthy to speak of the most holy mysteries of Love, I beseech Him to prompt my thoughts and my tongue so that I may be able to disclose to this excellent Courtier a love that lies beyond the practice of the common herd. And as I from boyhood have dedicated my whole life to him, now also may my words serve my purpose and his praise.

"I say then that since in youth human nature leans so strongly toward sense, sensual love may be conceded to the Courtier while he is young; but if afterward, in his maturer years as well, the Courtier happens to kindle with this love, he ought to be wary and guard against self-deception, not letting himself be drawn into those misfortunes that deserve more pity than blame in young men and more blame than pity in old men.

62. The first step upward on the stair of love consists in renouncing sensuality.

"Therefore, when he catches sight of some fine lady's gracious countenance accompanied by winning ways and courteous manners, and when as a man versed in the science of love he recognizes an affinity between his blood and her countenance—the very moment he perceives that his eyes seize upon her image and carry it to his heart, that his soul is beginning to dwell upon it with pleasure and to feel that influence which stirs and gradually warms his soul, and that those lively spirits which sparkle from her eyes are continually adding fuel to the fire: at this very first stage, he should apply some quick remedy, awakening his reason and arming with it the stronghold of his heart; and he should block up the paths against sense and the appetites so that these are unable to get in by force or deception.

"Thus, if the flame is extinguished, the danger also is extinguished; but if the fire persists or grows, then the Courtier, perceiving that he has been caught, should resolve to keep clear of every taint of ordinary love and set out on the path of divine love with reason as guide. And first he should reflect that the body in which the woman's beauty shines is not the source from which beauty springs but that on the contrary beauty, being something incorporeal and as we have said a divine ray, loses much of its worth when it is coupled with that vile and corruptible subject; for the more perfect beauty is the less it enters into that subject, being most perfect when entirely separate from it. He should further reflect that just as we cannot hear with the palate or smell with the ears, so also in no way can we through sense of touch enjoy beauty or satisfy the desire which beauty excites in our souls, but only through that sense of which beauty is the proper object, that is, the power of sight.

"Let him then abandon the blind judgment of sense and enjoy with his eyes that brilliance, that grace, those loving sparks, the laughter, the ways, and all the other attractive adornments of beauty; likewise let him through his hearing enjoy the sweetness of her voice, the melody of her speech, the harmony of the music she performs (if the woman he loves is a musician); and thus will he feed his soul most deliciously through means of these two senses which hold little of what is corporeal and which minister to the reason, without passing on to any appetite less than chaste through desire directed toward the body.

"Next let him wait upon, gratify, and with all reverence honor his lady, holding her dearer than his own self, placing her every comfort and wish before his own, and loving the beauty of her spirit no less than the beauty of her body. Therefore let him take care not to let her fall into any error but always try to lead her to continence, temperance, and true chastity by his admonitions and good counsel; and let him see to it that she harbors only thoughts that are spotless and free from the slightest taint of vice. And thus, by sowing virtue in the garden of that excellent mind, he will also gather the fruits of most excellent manners and relish them with wonderful delight: and this will constitute the true begetting of beauty in beauty, which some call the end of love.

"In such fashion will our Courtier greatly endear himself to his lady, and she will always be obliging, sweet, and amiable and as eager to please him as to be loved by him;

and the wishes of both will be entirely virutous and harmonious, and the lovers will consequently be extremely happy."

63. Are favors other than physical satisfactory rewards in love?

Here Messer Morello said:

"A real begetting of beauty in beauty would be the begetting of a fine child in a fine lady; and it would seem to me a much clearer token that she loved her lover if she gratified him with this than with that amiability which you speak of."

Bembo laughed and said:

"There is no need, Lord Morello, to get out of bounds; nor does the woman give insignificant tokens of love when she bestows her beauty on her lover and when, by the paths that form the passage to the soul, namely sight and hearing, she sends the glances of her eyes, the image of her countenance, her voice and her words, which penetrate to the lover's heart and bear witness of her love."

Said Lord Morello:

"Glances and words may be and often are false witnesses; hence a man who has no better pledge of love is, in my opinion, not well assured of it; and to tell the truth, I rather expected that you would make this lady of yours a little more gracious and generous towards the Courtier than the Magnifico has made his; but both of you seem to me to behave like those judges who pronounce sentence against their own side in order to appear wise."

64. Circumstances under which kissing is permissible.

Said Bembo:

"I do indeed wish this lady to be more gracious to my no longer youthful Courtier than the Lord Magnifico's is to his youthful one; and with reason, because mine desires only chaste things, and my lady can therefore grant them to him without reproach; whereas the Lord Magnifico's lady, who is not so sure of the young man's continence, ought to grant him only chaste wishes and deny him the unchaste. Therefore my lover, who is granted what he asks, is happier than the other who is granted part and denied part.

"And in order that you may understand even better that rational love is happier than sensual, I say that the very same things are sometimes to be denied in sensual love and granted in rational love, because in the former they are unchaste and in the latter chaste; therefore, in pleasing her virtuous lover, the lady, in addition to granting him amiable laughter, familiar and secret talk, wit, banter, and the touching of her hand, may with the approval of reason and without reproach go so far as kissing, which in sensual love is not permissible according to the rules of the Lord Magnifico; for inasmuch as kissing consists in a joining both of body with body and of soul with soul, there is the danger that the sensual lover may lean more toward the bodily than the spiritual side; whereas the rational lover recognizes that, while the mouth is of course a part of the body, none the less through it pass both words, which are interpreters of the soul, and that inward breath which is itself also called soul; and for this reason the lover delights in joining his mouth with the mouth of the woman he loves in a kiss, not in order to be excited to any unchaste desire but because he realizes that that bond opens the passage to the souls, which, drawn by mutual desire, are poured by turns from one body into the other and mingle in such fashion that each lover has two souls, and a single soul, composed thus of those two, sustains as it were two bodies; for which reason we can more justly call the kiss a union of soul than of body, because it has such power over the soul that it draws her to itself, and separates her from the body; for this reason all chaste lovers desire the kiss as spiritual union; and therefore Plato the divinely enamored says that in kissing his soul came to his lips in order to depart from his body. And because the separation of the soul from sensual things and her complete union with things intelligible can be signified by the kiss, Solomon says in his divine book, the *Song of Songs: Let him kiss me with the kiss of his mouth,* to express his desire that his soul may be transported by divine love to the contemplation of heavenly beauty, in such fashion that in uniting closely with it she may abandon the body."

65. Even chaste love of an individual woman entails suffering, however.

All were paying the closest attention to Bembo's discourse; and he, after making a brief pause, seeing that no one spoke, said:

"Since you have made me begin the revelation of happy love to our no longer youthful Courtier, I now want to lead him a little further forward; stopping at this point is extremely perilous, considering that the soul, as has been said more than once, leans strongly towards the senses; and even though reason by means of its discourse should make the right choice and, recognizing that beauty does not spring from the body, should therefore set a check on unchaste desires, still the everlasting contemplation of beauty in that body often perverts right judgment. And even when no other evil comes of it, absence from the loved object entails much suffering. For when beauty is present its influence gives a wonderful delight to the lover and by warming his heart awakens and melts certain powers which lie dormant and frozen in his soul. These, when they are nourished by the amorous warmth, circulate freely and go boiling up around the heart and send out through the eyes those spirits which are very fine vapors made of the purest, clearest part of the blood and which receive the image of beauty and deck it out in a thousand varied embellishments. By these the soul is delighted and with a kind of wonderment is at once frightened and yet rejoices and, as if bewildered, experiences along with pleasure that fear and reverence which she is accustomed to feel for sacred things, so that she thinks she is in very heaven.

66. *The lover must therefore love beauty in abstraction.*

"Therefore the lover who considers beauty only in the body, loses this blessing and this happiness as soon as the loved lady, by absenting herself, leaves his eyes bereft of their splendor and his soul consequently widowed of its blessings; for when beauty is absent that amorous influence does not warm the heart as it did when she was present. Therefore the pores are left arid and dry at the same time that the recollection of beauty stirs a little those powers of the soul, and they endeavor to set the vital spirits in circulation; and the latter, finding the passages stopped up, have no exit and yet try to escape and thus with their confined excitations sting the soul and cause her the sharpest suffering, as in children when the teeth begin to break through the tender gums. From this proceed the tears, sighs, sufferings and torments of lovers, because the soul continually grieves and suffers agony and almost goes mad, until that dear beauty appears before her once again; and then all at once she grows calm and breathes anew, and wholly intent upon that beauty feeds on sweetest food, nor would she ever want to leave a sight so charming.

"Therefore in order to avoid the torment of this absence and to enjoy beauty without suffering, the Courtier with reason's help must totally divert desire away from the body and to beauty alone, and to the best of his ability contemplate it in itself simple and unmixed; also in his imagination he must fashion it in abstraction from any matter whatsoever and thus render it friendly and precious to his soul and enjoy it there and keep it with him day and night, in every time and place, without fear of ever losing it; always calling to mind that the body is a thing quite unlike beauty and not only does not enhance beauty but diminishes its perfection. In this fashion the future Courtier who is no longer young will be safe from all the bitterness and the calamities which young men almost always experience, such as fits of jealousy, suspicion, scorn, anger, despair, and certain insane rages by which they are often led so far astray that some not only beat those ladies whom they love but even take their own lives.

"The Courtier will do no wrong to husband, father, brother, or kinsmen of his lady-love; he will not bring shame upon her; he will not be compelled to control his eyes and tongue, sometimes with great difficulty, in order not to betray to others his desires; he will not have to endure suffering over departures or absences; for he will always carry with him shut away in his heart his precious treasure; and also through power of imagination he will inwardly fashion that beauty far more beautiful than it actually is.

67. Mounting higher, the lover can learn to love the universal form of beauty.

"But among these blessings the lover will discover another much greater still, if he wishes to use this love as a step to mount to another much more exalted, as he will succeed in doing if he will always keep inwardly reflecting how narrow a bond it is, ever to be engaged in contemplating the beauty of one single body; and therefore, in order to escape this close confinement, he will little by little collect in his mind so many embellishments that, by heaping together all beauties, he will construct a universal concept and reduce the multitude of them to the unity of that single one which is spread generally over human nature; and thus he will no longer contemplate the particular beauty of one lady but that universal beauty which adorns all bodies.

"Then, blinded by this stronger light, he will not trouble himself over the lesser, and burning in a nobler flame he will little esteem the one which first he had so highly prized. This stage of love, thought very noble and such that few reach it, cannot however be called perfect, because the imagination, being an organic faculty and possessing no cognition except through those materials which are furnished it by the senses, is not completely purged of the shadows of materiality; and therefore, although it views that universal beauty abstracted and in itself, yet it does not discern it quite clearly, nor without a certain ambiguity caused by the resemblance which the phantasms bear to the body. Therefore those men who get as far as this love are like young birds which are just beginning to be covered with feathers and which, although they lift themselves a little in flight with weak wings, still do not dare go very far from the nest or commit themselves to the winds and the open sky.

*68. At the final stage there is awakening to
universal intellectual beauty.*

"When therefore our Courtier has arrived at this point, although he may be called a very happy lover in comparison with those who are sunk in the misery of sensual love, still I do not wish him to feel satisfied, but to move boldly forward, following along the lofty way behind the guide who leads him to the stage of the true bliss; and so, instead of going outside himself in thought, as one must who wishes to contemplate corporeal beauty, let him turn inward upon himself in order to contemplate that which is seen by the eyes of the mind, which begin to be sharp and discerning just when those of the body lose the flower of their beauty.

"Then the soul, divorced from vice, purged by the study of true philosophy, versed in spiritual life, and trained in matters of the understanding, turning to the contemplation of her own substance, as if awakened from deepest sleep, opens those eyes which all possess and few use, and sees in herself a ray of that light which is the true image of the angelic beauty imparted to her, of which she in turn imparts to the body a feeble shadow. Therefore, grown blind to earthly matters, she becomes very sharpsighted in celestial ones; and sometimes, when the motive powers of the body are held in abeyance by profound contemplation or are bound up by sleep, the soul, no longer hampered by them, is aware of a certain secret perfume of the true angelic beauty, and, enraptured by the splendor of that light, begins to catch fire, and follows it so eagerly that she almost becomes phrensied and beside herself, through desire to be united with it, seeming to have found the footstep of God, in the contemplation of which she seeks to rest as in her blessed end, and therefore, burning in this most happy flame, she rises to her noblest part, which is the understanding, where, darkened no longer by the deep night of terrestrial things, she beholds the divine beauty.

"But she does not yet enjoy it altogether perfectly, because she contemplates it only in her particular understanding, which cannot comprehend the vast universal beauty. Therefore love, not entirely content with this boon, gives the soul greater happiness; so that just as love guides her from the particular beauty of one body to the universal beauty of all bodies, so also it guides her in the final stage of perfection from the particular understanding to the universal understanding. Thus the soul, aflame with the most holy fire of true divine love, flies to unite herself with the angelic nature, and not only completely abandons sense, but has no further need of discourse of reason; so that transformed into an angel, she understands all things intelligible and beholds without veil or slightest cloud the wide sea of pure divine beauty and receives it into herself and enjoys that supreme happiness which cannot be grasped by the senses."

69. The supreme beauty is indistinguishable from the supreme good.

"If, then, the beauties which with these darkened eyes of ours we behold every day in corruptible bodies and which, however, are no more than dreams and thinnest shadows of beauty seem nevertheless to us so very lovely and charming that they oftentimes kindle in us the most intense fire and a delight so great that we think no happiness can equal the one which now and again we feel in a single glance that comes to us from the beloved eyes of a woman: what joyful wonder, what blessed amazement shall we think that may be which fills the souls that reach the vision of the divine beauty! What a sweet flame, what delicious burning must we believe that to be which rises from the spring of the supreme and true beauty!—which is the origin of every other beauty and which neither increases nor diminishes, always beautiful and in itself wholly pure as much in one part as in another; resembling only itself and deriving nothing by participation in any other, but beautiful in such a way that all other beautiful things are beautiful because they participate in its beauty.

"This is that beauty indistinguishable from the supreme good, which with its light calls and draws to itself all things, and not only imparts intellect to intellectual beings, reason to rational ones, and sense and the desire to live to sensual ones, but also communicates to plants and stones their motion and that natural instinct of their properties, as a vestige of itself. This love is therefore as much greater and more happy than others as the cause which moves it is more excellent; and therefore, just as the material fire refines gold, so this most holy fire in souls destroys and consumes what is mortal there and quickens and beautifies that heavenly part which sense earlier rendered lifeless and buried in them.

"This is the pyre on which, as the poets write, Hercules was burned on the summit of Mount Oeta and through that burning became after death divine and immortal; it is the burning briarbush of Moses, the divided tongues of fire, the flaming chariot of Elijah, which redoubles grace and felicity in the soul of those who are worthy enough to behold it when, taking leave of this earthly vileness, it soars toward heaven. Let us then direct all our thoughts and the powers of our soul toward this holiest light which shows us the path that leads to heaven, and in its wake, casting off the passions in which we clothed ourselves at our descent, by the stair which holds at its lower step the darkness of sensual love, let us ascend to the lofty abode where dwells the heavenly, adorable and true beauty, which lies hidden in the secret recesses of God so that unsanctified eyes cannot behold it; and there we shall find the happiest end to our longings, true repose amid toils, certain relief in sufferings, medicine most salutary in sickness, and safest of harbors in the blustering storms of this life's tempestuous sea.

70. Bembo prays for the supreme enlightenment.

"What mortal tongue shall there be then, O love most holy, which can praise you adequately? Loveliest, best, wisest, you proceed from the union of divine beauty and goodness and wisdom, and in that union you remain, and to it, through it, as in a circle you return. Most pleasant bond of the world, mediator between heaven and earthly things, with kindly tempering you bend the higher powers to the government of the inferior ones, and by turning the minds of mortals back to their source unite them with it. You bind together the elements in harmony and impel nature to bring to birth, and what is born you impel to the cycle of life. You unite things dissevered and bestow perfection on things imperfect, likeness on things unlike, friendship on things inimical, fruits on the earth, calm on the sea, life-giving light on the heavens.

"You are father of true pleasures, of graces, of peace, of gentleness and benevolence, hostile to rustic fierceness and to sloth—in short, source and end of every good. And because you love to dwell in the bloom of beautiful bodies and beautiful souls and from that place sometimes reveal yourself a little to the eyes and to the minds of those who are worthy of beholding you, I believe that you now are abiding among us here. Therefore be pleased, Lord, to hear our prayers; pour yourself into our hearts and light up our darkness with the refulgence of your holiest fire; and like a trusted guide in this blind maze show us the true path. Correct the deceptions of the senses, and after our prolonged pursuit of vanities give us the true and solid good; cause us to smell those spiritual odors which quicken the powers of the understanding and to hear the celestial music which is so harmonious that no discord of passion shall have a place in us ever again; make us drunk at that inexhaustible spring of contentment which always delights and never cloys and which to one who drinks its living and lucid waters gives a taste of true blessedness; with your beams cleanse our eyes of cloudy ignorance so that we may no longer prize mortal beauty and may realize that the things which our eyes first seem to see are not and that those which they do not see, truly are. Accept our souls which we offer to you in sacrifice; burn them in that living flame which consumes all the material grossness, so that, being wholly freed from the body, they may be united with the divine beauty through everlasting and most delectable bonds and we, estranged from ourselves, be able to transform ourselves into the loved one as true lovers should, and by raising ourselves from earth be admitted to the feast of the angels, where, fed on immortal ambrosia and nectar, we at last die by a most happy and lively death, as formerly died those ancient fathers, whose soul by the most intense power of contemplation you ravished away from the body and united with God. . . ."

71. Emilia recalls Bembo from his ecstasy.

After Bembo had spoken up to this point with such fervor that he almost seemed transported and beside himself, he stood silent and still, with his eyes raised toward heaven like one bereft of his wits; whereupon Lady Emilia, who with the rest had been listening most attentively to the discourse, took hold of him by the fold of his gown and shaking him a little said:

"Be careful, Messer Pietro, that in company with these thoughts your soul also does not take leave of your body."

"Madame," answered Messer Pietro, "that would not be the first miracle that love has worked in me."

Thereupon the Duchess and all the others began anew

to urge Bembo to continue, and each seemed as it were to feel in his own soul a certain spark of that divine love which prompted the speaker, and all wanted to hear more. But Bembo replied:

"I have spoken what the sacred madness of love has dictated to me at the moment; now that it seems not to inspire me further, I should not know what to say. And I think love is not willing that his secrets be further revealed or that the Courtier go beyond that stage which it has pleased love that I should show him; and therefore it is perhaps not lawful to speak further about this subject."

72. Are women as well as men capable of divine love?

"Truly," said the Duchess, "if the no longer youthful Courtier is such that he can follow the road which you have shown him, in all reason he ought to be contented with so great a happiness and not envy the young man."

Then Messer Cesare Gonzaga said:

"The road which leads to this happiness looks to me so steep that I find difficulty in believing that anyone could travel it."

Lord Gaspar added:

"To travel it would, I believe, be difficult for men, but for women impossible."

Lady Emilia laughed and said:

"Lord Gaspar, if you return so often to doing us wrong, I promise you that I shall not pardon you any more."

Lord Gaspar replied:

"No one does you wrong in saying that the souls of women are not so thoroughly cleansed of the passions as the souls of men, nor so learned in contemplation as Messer Pietro has said those must be which want to taste divine love. Furthermore, we do not read that any woman has received this grace, but many men certainly have, such as Plato, Socrates, and Plotinus and many others, and among us so many holy fathers, such as Saint Francis, on whom a burning spirit of love imprinted the most holy seal of the five wounds. Nor would any other power than that of love have been able to carry Saint Paul up to the vision of those secrets of which it is unlawful for man to speak; nor to show Saint Stephen the heavens opened."

Here the Magnifico Giuliano replied:

"In this respect women will not in the least be outdone by men. For Socrates himself acknowledged that all the mysteries of love that he knew were revealed to him by a woman, who was that certain Diotima. And the angel who wounded Saint Francis with the fire of love has also made several women of our era worthy of the same mark. You ought also to recall that many sins were forgiven Saint Mary Magdalene because she loved much, and with no less gift of grace than Saint Paul's she was many times transported to the third heaven by angelic love; and you ought to recall very many other women who, as I narrated more at large yesterday, through the love of the name of Christ have not valued their lives or feared suffering or any sort of death however horrible and cruel it might be, and who were not old, as Messer Pietro wishes his Courtier to be, but tender and delicate maids and of that age at which he says sensual love should be countenanced in men."

73. The discussion is concluded at dawn.

Lord Gaspar was getting himself ready to answer; but the Duchess said:

"Let Messer Bembo be judge of this and let his verdict be accepted, whether or not women are as capable of divine love as men are. But because the contest between you might last too long, it will be well to defer it to tomorrow."

"Rather to this evening," said Messer Cesare Gonzaga.

"Why to this evening?" said the Duchess.

Messer Cesare replied:

"Because it is already day."

And he showed her the light that was beginning to enter through the chinks of the windows. Thereupon everyone stood up with great surprise, because it did not appear that the discourses could have lasted longer than usual; but because they began much later and proved most charming they had so beguiled those lords that the flight of the hours had not been perceived, nor was there anyone whose eyes felt heavy with sleepiness as almost always happens when we stay awake beyond the customary hour of sleep. When the windows were thereupon opened on that side of the palace which faces the high summit of Mt. Catri, they saw a beautiful rose-colored dawn already sprung in the east and the stars all vanished except that sweet mistress of the heaven of Venus, which stands on the boundary between night and day. From it there seemed to breathe a gentle gust which, in filling the air with a nipping coolness, began to waken sweet songs of the delightful birds among the rustling woods on the hillsides nearby. Then all having respectfully taken leave of the Duchess, they departed in the direction of their apartments without light of torches, the light of day sufficing.